RALPH FLETCHER

THE *Writing Teacher's* COMPANION

Embracing Choice, Voice, Purpose & Play

SCHOLASTIC

CREDITS

Stock photos ©: cover: Klaus Vedfelt/Getty Images; 25: AzmanJaka/iStockphoto; 94–95: gradyreese/iStockphoto. All other photos by James Flanagan, Ralph Fletcher, JoAnn Portalupi, Mike Reynolds, Megan Sloan, Ronna Zigmand.

"Houston" by Ralph Fletcher. Copyright © 2017 by Ralph Fletcher. Published by Scholastic Inc. *Grandpa Never Lies* by Ralph Fletcher, illustrated by Harvey Stevenson. Text copyright © 2000 by Ralph Fletcher. Illustrations copyright © 2000 by Harvey Stevenson. Used by permission of Marian Reiner on behalf of the author and by Shannon Associates, LLC. "A Writing Kind of Day" by Ralph Fletcher from *A Writing Kind of Day*. Text copyright © 2005 by Ralph Fletcher. Used by permission of Boyds Mills Press. "The Experiment" by DeAndre Porter. Published by Scholastic Inc. Used by permission. "Mauled by Seagulls" by Peter Lee. Published by Scholastic Inc. Used by permission. "The Good Old Days" adapted from "Bedtime" by Ralph Fletcher from *Relatively Speaking*. Text copyright © 1999 by Ralph Fletcher. Published by Scholastic Inc. Used by permission of Marian Reiner on behalf of the author.

Publisher/Acquiring editor: Lois Bridges
Production editor: Danny Miller
Cover designer: Brian LaRossa
Interior designer: Maria Lilja

ISBN-13: 978-1-338-14804-6

6 2021

ACKNOWLEDGMENTS

Lois Bridges was the driving force behind this book. She and I have worked together on and off for 20-some years. I'm grateful for her kindness, wisdom, and unflinching support.

Kudos to the team at Scholastic who brought this book to life: Ray Coutu, Brian LaRossa, Sarah Longhi, Danny Miller, Maria Lilja, and Suzanne Akceylan.

I am particularly thankful to several remarkable writing teachers who generously provided classroom photos for this book: Ann Marie Corgill, Megan Sloan, and Mike Reynolds.

A book like this takes months to write, but that time frame is deceiving. Think of this book as a tree with an elaborate root system both wide and deep, one that has evolved and spread for many years. I'm grateful for all the colleagues who have enriched my thinking on writing. The list of these individuals includes (but is not limited to) Jennifer Allen, Carl Anderson, Maureen Barbieri, Lucy Calkins, Kathy Collins, Ruth Culham, Kathleen Fay, Dan Feigelson, Matt Glover, Jane Hansen, Shelley Harwayne, Georgia Heard, Martha Horn, Penny Kittle, Ann Marie Krier, Barry Lane, Tom Newkirk, Holly Price, Katie Wood Ray, Linda Rief, Stacy Shubitz, Philippa Stratton, Tom Romano, Franki Sibberson, Ladd Tobin, Suzanne Whaley, and Cyrene Wells.

Several educators provided quotes for the chapter openers. Mega-thanks to Jeff Anderson, Katherine Bomer, Kelly Gallagher, and Jen Serravallo.

Like many other educators, I will always walk in the big shoes worn by "the Dons"—Don Graves and Don Murray.

I couldn't have written this book without JoAnn Portalupi, a true companion in every sense of the word.

Table of Contents

Introduction

It begins with a blank page... the empty computer screen. What will you write today? That tingle at the base of your spine is excitement mixed with nervousness.

It begins with an empty classroom. Gazing out at all the unoccupied desks, you feel spasms of anticipation and edginess in equal measure. What kind of classroom will you create this year? The possibilities (as well as the pitfalls) seem almost infinite.

Building a strong writing workshop may seem like a daunting task. Recently a new teacher told me she found the idea of running a writing workshop to be overwhelming. But it doesn't have to be. You've got this! And I'm excited to support you in any way I can. *Companion* is the most important word in the title of this book. Don Murray once said that the best books on writing help us "see through the complexities to the underlying simplicities." I hope to do that here. Through this book I hope to become a professional friend and diminish the sense of isolation that so many teachers feel.

Teaching writing is fun, sure enough, but it's hard work, too. That's because writing isn't one skill but a bundle of skills: sequencing, spelling, elaborating, and transitioning from one paragraph to another, just to name a few. A writing teacher needs a bundle of skills to nourish young writers. Some of these skills are social: knowing when to praise, nudge, or look the other way. Some rely on an understanding of writing itself. Still others depend on your evolving understanding of the individual students in your class.

I deliberately constructed these chapters so they would be short, punchy, and digestible. Everybody is time-starved—no sense in spooling out long, windy chapters nobody has time to read.

Choice runs like a silver thread through the fabric of my professional work, so it's not surprising to find it here. I want you to exercise choice in how you teach writing. I believe that your workshop must reflect your personality, quirks, strengths, and preferences. This is anything but a rigid, follow-the-recipe cookbook for teaching writing. I encourage you to improvise and go off script if the situation warrants it, to make your writing classroom a reflection of who you are. In writing this book, I imagined each of these chapters as an invitation to a room. The doors are open and unlocked, but it's up to you to decide if, when, and how to step through. **Teachers are notoriously time-crunched. To make this book as reader-friendly as possible, I have highlighted (in a blue background) what I consider the most important part of each chapter.**

I've been teaching writing for more than 30 years, and have written many books on this subject, for teachers as well as kids. You'll find a ton of practical information for setting up your workshop, troubleshooting the rough parts, and keeping the energy high (theirs AND yours). But I want to do more than that. I want this book to serve as sustenance for the writing teacher's soul (if that doesn't sound too hokey). I hope these pages will give you support and encouragement as you strive to nourish the young writers in your class, and create a place where they can thrive. It's your journey, but I'm happy to walk with you. We'll walk together, side by side.

PART ONE

Attitudes That Foster Writing

Every child can write.

—DONALD GRAVES

Keep It Simple

Your students need to write every day.

That's it. That's the gist of this book. In later pages, we'll look at specific steps we can take to help our students become strong, confident writers. We'll explore the who, what, where, when, and why of writing. But let's linger on this idea for a few moments and not rush ahead. It's easy to overcomplicate matters, to bury important truths beneath a blizzard of verbiage. I don't want to do that now.

Your students need to write every day.

What would you do if you hoped to help your son learn to speak Spanish? I don't mean to pick up a few words or phrases—I mean to become fluent enough to use Spanish in his life. Would you sign him up for an occasional Spanish class? That's not enough; he'd need a lot more than that. Ideally, you'd arrange for him to spend a summer in Costa Rica, Mexico, or Spain, where he could hang out with other kids his age. Okay, that might not be feasible, but at the very least you'd make sure that he spends lots of time in an environment where he could interact with Spanish speakers. That would give him the opportunity to use Spanish for real purposes every day.

Writing is no different. Your students need to write every day. Writing should be one of the foundational beams of your classroom. Not a decorative beam, but a weight-bearing wall.

Here's a little secret that may surprise you: It's not so much that you will teach your kids to write. They will teach themselves by writing every day, and by living in a community of writers.

Ralph on Writing
scholastic.com/
WritingCompanion
Resources

Even with a "bad" piece of writing,
a good teacher will reach into the chaos,
find a place where the writing works,
pull it from the wreckage, name it,
and make the writer aware of his or her
emerging skill with words.

—R.F.

Helpful Attitudes: Yours

Camels drink up water and store it in their humps before beginning a long journey. Okay, so what provisions should you pack in your hump as you prepare for the long trek from September to June? Make sure to pack your:

- **Sense of humor.** Expect to laugh a lot because kids' writing can be delightful. Even their mistakes can be pretty hysterical. I always look forward to that when I meet with young writers, knowing for certain that my funny bone will get tickled.

Letter from a student to me

> Dear Ralph Fletcher,
>
> I really enjoyed reading your books. They were fun, easy, and full of themes. We did a prodject on both Fig Pudding and Marshfield Dreams. I wish you could see them. My favorite one so far out of Marshfield Dreams, Fig Pudding, and Flying Solo would be Flying Solo. It is a really funny, exciting, and full of themes.

- **Sense of adventure.** You and your students are embarking on a voyage, and a true journey always contains unexpected twists and turns. As a writing teacher, you start with a rough idea of which direction you want to take, but the only true maps are sketchy ones containing lots of unexplored territory.

- **Sense of curiosity.** Strong writing feels personal because it is. Your students' daily writing will give you a window into who they are. It will give you a unique opportunity to get to know each one of them—their passions, quirks, obsessions—like nothing else in the curriculum.

It has been said that having expectations can be dangerous, and perhaps that's true, but I believe you should go into the school year with your eyes wide open. Be realistic. You'll have a much smoother year if you expect:

- **Imperfection.** Sorry, but you won't be the perfect writing teacher. On some days you'll just be "off"— and so will they. Cut yourself some slack in this regard.

- **Flashes of brilliance.** You'll find them when you least expect it, rare little rubies in your students' writing, moments when you want to exclaim: "Hey everybody! Listen to this!" Be alert so you can seize upon those moments when they arise.

- **Energy fluctuations.** On certain days you'll be more up than on others. Don't punish yourself for days when you can feel your energy flagging. And pay attention to what seems to be sapping your energy.

- **Diversity, not conformity.** Creating 26 identical writing clones is most certainly NOT the goal. Each of your students is unique, and you want to do everything you can to encourage that uniqueness.

Remember: You tap into the strength of a community when you tap into its diversity.

○ **On-the-job-training. Don't expect to have it all figured out ahead of time because that ain't gonna happen. You'll learn as you go.** And what you learn—from trial and error, from your peers, from attending educational conferences, from professional reading, from your students, their writing, and your interactions with them—will make you a stronger writing teacher by the end of the year.

Talking to students about writing

I'm writing—please join me.

—(WHAT TEACHER/AUTHOR JANET EMIG
WROTE ON THE BOARD AT THE
BEGINNING OF WRITING CLASS)

3

Write With Your Students

What do you do while your kids are writing? The answer is simple: **write along with them. By doing so you give them a rare gift: They can look up to see their teacher engaged in the same process (musing, noodling, drafting, crossing out, adding, starting again) that they're wrestling with.**

Young readers need to see adults they admire engaged in reading. If they never see adults reading, well, how important could it possibly be? The same principle holds true for writing.

Write with your students. I'm not talking about a half hour of sustained writing. That's probably not feasible. Plus, you'll want to devote a chunk of time to conferring with your students while they're in the act of writing (see Chapter 14). But there's no reason why you can't take the first five to seven minutes to work on a piece of your own writing. Doing so will have several benefits:

- It will settle the class and set a serious tone.
- It's powerful modeling.
- It will encourage independence. If you're writing, it's less likely that they'll interrupt. This signals to students that they cannot always expect you to solve their problems.

- It will allow you to have authentic writing (yours) to share with the class.

- It lets you sample the vibe in the workshop. Is there a supportive environment, or are snarky comments commonplace? Writing and sharing your own writing is the best way to know for sure.

- Writing with your students builds sweat equity in the tone/ambience of the workshop. Instead of saying "I want you to be quiet," you earn the right to ask, "What kind of environment do we need so we can all do our best writing?"

Write with your students. I won't lie to you—it's a major commitment, one that requires a significant shift in how you see your role. But it will pay surprising dividends. Writing alongside your students will change the dynamic in the classroom, particularly in regard to discipline. Instead of saying what teachers have said since forever—"I expect you to write"—you are signaling to them: "Let's create a time and space where we can all write together. It's got to work for you, and it's got to work for me, as well."

Writing with your kids is a way of rolling up your sleeves and getting into the game. It makes you a co-conspirator. It's a way of letting them know that you have skin in the game, too.

Be forewarned: It can be humbling to write with your kids. When you teach first grade, the chances are quite good that you're the strongest writer in the class. However, by fifth grade, you may have students who amaze and surpass you. If you teach eighth, ninth, or tenth grade, it's quite likely you'll have one or more students who can write better than you. That's okay. Swallow your pride and write alongside them.

Idea for a novel
   (sort of about my life)

Big family — lots of kids

Title ideas: 1) From Christmas
                    to Christmas
              2) Gifts of the season
              3) ?

Include

  * Jimmy collecting junk

  * Biting heads off marshmallow chicks

  * Christmas Cactus

  * Death of a kid (too sad ?)

  * Under the kitchen table

  * Grandma Annie

  * New baby ?

Narrator — should be oldest kid

Time frame ?

**Pages from my own
writer's notebook**

The moon scatters silvery coins
~~on the~~ over the lakes and ponds and seas...

Something is stirring ✗
at the edge of the world.

Something is rising
low in the trees.

(lunatic comes from lunar !)

Like a celestial shortstop
the moon catches light
from the sun
        and throws it
              to the earth

Moonshine, moonlight
be sure to wear your "moon screen"
so you don't get
"moon-burned" tonight!

    Neil Armstrong —
        first person to walk on the moon

Did ancestors pray to the moon ?
    Did they fear it ?

It's knowing how a writer feels when a piece is shared, the chemical twang, the mental involvement, the "I'm out there and feeling vulnerable" sensations that you must comprehend if you want to do a decent teaching job.

—RUTH NATHAN ON WHY WRITING
TEACHERS NEED TO WRITE

4

A Writer-With-a-Small-w

"Are you a photographer?" the woman sitting next to me asked.

I paused before answering. I was heading to Costa Rica for a 10-day nature photography trip. In the overhead compartment, I had stowed a roller bag containing all my photography equipment. I had a macro lens, photography book, two camera manuals, plus an issue of *Popular Photography* jammed into my carry bag. So why did I hesitate?

"I'm, uh, well, I'm learning," I finally said. "I'm a serious amateur."

It's curious that I was so reluctant to claim my status. While I'm certainly not a Photographer à la Ansel Adams or Richard Avedon, it's fair to say that I'm a photographer. But when it came to defining myself in that way, to say it out loud, I held back. Many folks do a similar thing when it comes to writing.

"Are you a writer?"

"Uh, no." Nervous smile. "Well, you know, yeah, I fool around a little. I mean, I like to write for myself, but I've never published anything."

That last comment is telling. Many people seem to believe that unless they make money at an activity—as a certified professional—they can't claim their status as a writer.

Imagine Maureen, a woman who is a terrific cook. She reads *Gourmet* and *Bon Appétit* from cover to cover. Her TV is permanently turned to the cooking channel. Her cabinets contain dozens of exotic spices you've never even heard of. She has dinner parties to die for. You want to weep after you swallow the last delectable bite.

Is it necessary for Maureen to open a bistro at the edge of town in order to certify herself as a cook? Heck, no. The woman loves cooking, does it all the time, and takes enormous pleasure in it. Anyone who knows Maureen knows that cooking is a big part of her identity. Who cares if Maureen is a Cook or a cook—her food is incredible! In a similar way, your students won't care if you're a (published) Writer, but they will be very aware of whether or not you're a writer-with-a-small-w. That's a standard all of us can meet.

Writing with your students really is a game-changer. It will impact almost everything: how you set up the room, how you confer with your students, how you structure a share session. It is a well you'll draw upon again and again.

I've talked about how important it is to write alongside them, but it's equally important to share the writing you do in the rest of your life: creating a poem for your father's 75th birthday, formulating a complaint letter, etc. Show your students that writing does heavy lifting in your life. Sharing yourself as a writer is a powerful way to communicate:

- Writing is important to me.
- I'm also trying to improve my writing.
- I'm in it for the long haul.
- Writing is an activity I find challenging, but I'm willing to work hard at it because I find it meaningful.
- Writing gives me pleasure—it's fun!

I can't dunk a basketball…
not even close…but sometimes
when I'm writing I feel like
I'm soaring above the rim.

—EVERETT, FIFTH GRADER

5

Helpful Attitudes: Theirs

Your students' attitudes about writing will permeate your classroom. Each of your students has already been shaped by innumerable writing experiences—praise, criticism, tedious assignments, the time she won a poetry contest, etc.

You can't control students' attitudes on writing, but you can certainly influence them. And that's important, because how they feel about writing will go a long way toward determining whether or not they are successful.

Attitudes about writing will affect student achievement, and they will strongly impact the feel of your writing classroom. At the beginning of the school year, a teacher friend of mine (Kate) invited a group of fifth graders to imagine what it would be like to spend a week skiing.

"Awesome!" Gunther blurted. "I love skiing, and I'm wicked good at it. I'm, like, Olympic-quality."

"I don't ski," Philomena muttered. "I don't think I'd like it."

"Never tried it," Omar admitted. "I'd be kind of nervous, at first."

"Do you think it would be scary?" Kate prompted. "Possibly terrifying?"

Some kids nodded; others shook their heads.

"Most ski mountains have different kind of trails," Kate put in. "There are green circle trails (easy), blue square trails (moderate), diamond trails (steep, difficult), and double-diamond (very difficult)."

"I love double-diamonds!" Gunther blurted. "Except when you wipe out because when that happens it's: GARAGE SALE!"

Rhonda made air quotes with her fingers. "What's a 'garage sale'"?

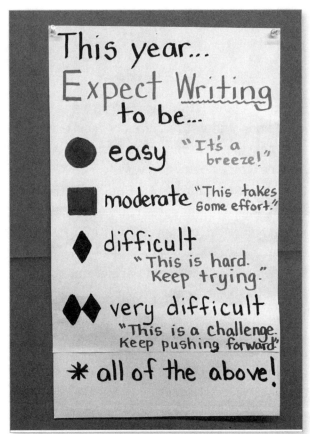

(from Megan Sloan's third-grade classroom in Snohomish School District, WA)

"That's when you're skiing real fast," Gunther said, "and you fall and your equipment goes flying in every direction."

"Cool!" Ryan exclaimed.

"The writing you do this year will be like that," Kate explained. "There will be lots of different 'slopes' and challenges. Some will be easy, some will be harder. Don't expect perfection. I won't expect it, either. Some days you'll write like a champ—on other days you'll wipe out. When that happens, get up, brush yourself off, and try again. I only ask that you give it your best shot. Anyway, I can promise you one thing: It's going to be fun."

She gave the kids a moment to digest that, and then added: "Your writing will be one of the ways I get to know who you are. I can't wait to see what you write."

Early on it's important to give your students a clear, unambiguous message that you are interested in them as writers. You want to get them thinking: *This sounds pretty good. I think I can write for this teacher.*

You can't change their previous writing experiences, but you can let them know that this year things will be different. This year writing is going to be fun. Of course, it's not enough to simply say that. That's a promise you need to deliver on. This may sound wildly optimistic, but I've seen it happen many times: With the encouragement of a strong teacher, a turned-off kid can turn him or herself into a writer.

Write about what makes you different.

—SANDRA CISNEROS

6

An Environment That Encourages Risk

I had been invited to work with some gifted writers at a high school in Maine. A few days before my visit, I sent their teacher a sampling of my writing, including one poem that began like this:

Houston

At the Holiday Inn I look out
past the bright aorta of traffic
to the Houston Medical Center
where fifteen years ago
Michael Debakey opened my father's chest...

Later, when I showed up at the high school, I asked the students what they thought of my poem.

"What about that line: *the bright aorta of traffic,*" I said. "Does that work? Or am I trying too hard?"

One tall boy raised his hand.

"To tell you the truth, I think you're trying too hard in all your writing."

Ouch. Even after all the books I have published, a comment like that stings. That's because writing is personal. When we write, and share that writing, we really do make ourselves vulnerable.

We put ourselves on the line. But we will continue doing that only if it feels like a safe place.

It's up to you to make sure that the classroom environment is supportive. You have to monitor the temperature in this regard. You can take active steps to make your workshop a safe writing space by:

- sharing writing of your own about a personal topic where you feel vulnerable.
- respecting a student who opts not to share.
- modeling supportive responses.

During a share session some students ask questions that come across as unfriendly or even aggressive; they may need guidance in asking supportive questions that are helpful to the writer. After a student reads his or her writing, other students might respond like this:

This seems to be about…

I really connected to the part where…

I wanted to know more about…

Statements that begin like this still give the writer helpful information without carrying the barbed hook of judgment.

I've noticed that when it comes to being supportive, the student with a high IQ may not necessarily have a high EQ (emotional intelligence). I spent time in one classroom where the brightest kid (according to the teacher) was certainly the most negative. One girl shared a story about the grief she felt when her best friend moved away.

"Oh, how *touching*," he said, sarcastically rolling his eyes.

Stop right there. Negative, snarky comments like that cannot stand. They are destructive in any classroom, but particularly so during writing where people are (hopefully) expressing issues that are personal in nature. Nobody will share if students are allowed to make such remarks like this. And their writing will suffer as well; kids will tend to choose generic subjects they don't really care about, but won't leave them vulnerable to ridicule.

Establishing a supportive tone seems like a no-brainer, and yet I have worked with some educators who aren't convinced.

"I don't go for that kumbaya stuff," one principal told me. "Life is tough. I don't think we do these kids any favor by coddling them."

I responded by sharing a concept I learned from Nancy Steineke—"home court advantage." She borrows this term from the world of sports, a realm not exactly known for being touchy-feely.

"Sports teams win more games at home than away because of home court advantage," Steineke points out. "When you play at home, the crowd is really pulling for you and it makes a huge difference. That's the same advantage we want to create in the classroom. When we work together, we are each other's teammates—and each other's fans."

Writers from Mike Reynolds' third-grade classroom at Chestnutwold School, Ardmore, PA

PART TWO

Writing Workshop: Getting Started

Write only what you love,
and love what you write.
The key word is love.
You have to get up in the
morning and write something
you love, something to live for.

—RAY BRADBURY

7

Commonsense Thinking About Goals

In the beginning of the school year a writing teacher should focus on:

SHORT-TERM GOALS

- Make sure your writers are engaged.
- Make sure they love writing time.
- Create a safe environment where kids can take risks.
- Establish predictable routines and a workable management system.
- Find out who your students are as writers.

Throughout the school year a writing teacher should focus on:

LONG-TERM GOALS

- Help students improve the quality of their writing.
- Build students' concept of strong writing.
- Model yourself as a writer-with-a-small-*w*.

Ralph on Writing
scholastic.com/
WritingCompanion
Resources

- Make sure students explore their passions through their writing.
- Provide opportunities for them to share and celebrate their writing in both big and small ways.
- Help them become problem-solvers: recognizing what's working in their writing, what's not working, and having options to solve their problems.
- Help them make deeper connections between what they read and what they write.
- Build their knowledge about various genres—not only the distinctions between genres but also the commonalities.
- Deepen their understanding of what writers do (process) when they write.
- Help them become more skilled at rereading their rough drafts.

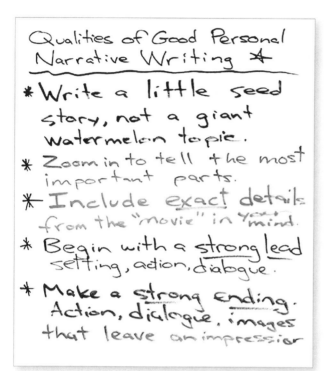

Qualities of Good Personal
Narrative Writing ✱
* Write a little seed
  story, not a giant
  watermelon topic.
* Zoom in to tell the most
  important parts.
* Include exact details
  from the "movie" in your mind.
* Begin with a strong lead
  setting, action, dialogue.
* Make a strong ending.
  Action, dialogue, images
  that leave an impression

Teachers and students can draft their own goals for their writing

(from Mike Reynolds' third-grade classroom at Chestnutwold School, Ardmore, PA)

Raise the Quality
of your writing!
* Free write for   SMALL ⤳
  specifics.   DETAILS
* Make a Mind
  Picture
* Try a Golden Line.   (had got went is)
* Use Strong Verbs.
  Use precise nouns.   (thing stuff)
* Show, don't tell.
* Slow down the "Hot Spot!"
* Start near the
  End near it too.   Remember:
                      You want to
        ☺   hear the
                      waterfall.

Writing is waiting for a place to happen. We create that space in our classrooms.

—JEFF ANDERSON

8

Creating a Writing Space

A story contains three basic elements: characters, plot, and setting—the same elements that can be found in your classroom. The characters (your students) and plot (their writing) may seem like the most important elements in the "story" you're creating. But the setting—the physical classroom—will matter more than you think.

I do most of my writing in my upstairs office at home, looking out at trees and birds. It's a quiet neighborhood. Occasionally a posse of wild turkeys will make their way across the yard, but otherwise there's not much to disturb my concentration, which is how I like it. When I'm away from home, I prefer to write in public places, such as a library or coffee shop. You'll find me sitting next to a tall window spilling in natural light. I find comfort in being able to hear the hiss of the latte machine, the white noise of human conversation, while at the same time knowing I won't be interrupted since I'm among strangers.

It's probably not feasible to import a latte machine to your classroom, but when it comes to the physical environment, you'll have some important decisions to make. What kind of feng shui do you hope to create?

When it comes to designing the classroom, some teachers solicit their students' input. That's an intriguing idea; I do admire that collaborative spirit. However, first and foremost, the classroom setup must work for *you*. You have to feel comfortable with it. There's no template; I've seen many different kinds of workable arrangements. Here are a few things to consider:

- **Meeting area.** You'll want a space where you can pull kids together for a pep talk, for a read-aloud, and to share their writing. Get a comfortable rug and unroll it in a part of the room (the back, or a corner) where there will be a minimum of distractions.

- **Desk arrangements.** You'll find it easier to talk/confer with individual students if you cluster student desks in groups of three or four. I find that long rows of desks aren't conducive to writing conferences.

- **Materials Center.** You don't want your students running up every few minutes interrupting you to ask for paper, scissors, etc. It makes sense to create some kind of writing center where students can go to get what they need. You don't need a lot of commercial material. A workable writing center might contain:

  - papers (a variety of sizes)

  - markers, crayons, scissors

  - dictionary and thesaurus

  - writing folders

  Organize the Materials Center to encourage independence. I know teachers who prefer clear bins so kids can quickly see what's inside and find the material they need. Some teachers like to have one central place in the classroom; others use a caddy that can be placed on each cluster of desks. Spend a few minutes explaining about the Writing Center, and how kids should use it.

- **Classroom library.** You'll want a place for the books you use as mentor texts. And don't forget a shelf to hold the books your students produce.

There's no perfect way to set up a classroom. Every teacher is different; the physical space should reflect your personality and preferences. The arrangement of desks, chairs, rugs, etc., will reflect your underlying values. Do you want a hushed, solemn ambience, or are you willing to live with a certain amount of movement and activity?

The physical classroom provides another opportunity for choice to manifest itself. Bottom line: You want each student to feel "at home" in your classroom when they are writing. By this I mean that they should feel comfortable using the space as they choose to use it. Some of them will prefer to work quietly at their desk. Others will want to lie on the rug and write on paper backed by a clipboard. Still others will retreat to a hidden corner. The classroom setup should be flexible enough to accommodate your students' quirks and preferences so they'll have the optimal conditions to produce strong writing.

There are many options for creating areas in the classroom that encourage writing.

(from Megan Sloan's third-grade classroom in Snohomish School District, WA)

This is how you do it:
You sit down at the keyboard
and you put one word after
another until it's done.
It's that easy, and that hard.

—NEIL GAIMAN

9

Making Time

Time is a new kind of poverty. Seems like everyone is running short. Everybody feels the squeeze. Look at the ludicrous way we lurch from one activity to another. In early morning the day starts to get ahead of us, and we never manage to catch up. Who among us could say we spend ample time on what we truly want to do?

Teachers feel the time-crunch every day, spending way too much time on a list of "we-have-to" activities, and not nearly enough on the "I-want-to" or "I-love-to" time that brought us into teaching in the first place.

Planning writing time may conjure up stress, but that can't be avoided. Your daily classroom schedule is more than a matter of practicality. It also reflects your underlying value system. Teachers who schedule writing only sporadically are, in effect, telling students: "Writing really isn't all that important to me...otherwise we'd be doing it more often."

On the other hand, a schedule that features daily writing communicates to students: "Writing is one of my non-negotiables. It's too important for me to squeeze in once in a blue moon."

The writing workshop takes 45 to 60 minutes per day. Although there's no single way to run a workshop, most teachers embrace a structure that looks something like this:

5–7 minutes   pep talk or mini-lesson

30–40 minutes   sustained writing time

10–12 minutes   share time

How should these three be ranked in order of value? Many teachers plan as if the mini-lesson is what matters most, but I would rank sustained writing time as the most important, by far.

March 20, 2017
3 - 20 - 17
Monday

8:30 Read to Self
9:00 Readers Workshop
10:25 Music

11:00 Writing Workshop
11:50 Lunch
12:45 Story
1:05 Math
2:00 Recess
2:15 Science
3:15 Dismissal

A schedule that features daily writing communicates to students: "Writing is one of my non-negotiables. It's too important for me to squeeze in once in a blue moon."

(from Megan Sloan's third-grade classroom in Snohomish School District, WA)

Your students need to write daily, or four times a week, or, at the very least, three times a week. That's where I draw my line in the sand. Look for a time slot with a minimum of outside interruptions. Put writing in your daily class schedule, and jealously protect that time. If students know when they'll be writing next they can do what writers do. They can look ahead, anticipate, and mentally compose (rehearse) even when it's not writing time.

Malcolm Gladwell famously argued that an individual must invest 10,000 hours learning and practicing a skill in order to become proficient. That number may be arbitrary but his underlying premise rings true. Your students need to spend a great deal of time writing in order to learn how to write well. There's no quick fix or shortcut. Schedule ample time for that to happen.

In some schools, teachers and administrators do a great deal of "talking about" writing, but it's little more than lip service. In other schools, educators create classrooms where kids actually write on a regular basis. Let's make that the gold standard.

*Keep a small can of WD-40
on your desk—away from any open
flames—to remind yourself
that if you don't write daily,
you'll get rusty.*

—GEORGE SINGLETON

10

The Concept of Ongoingness

Mrs. Savage always dropped her writing assignments on Monday morning. In this case it was a four-page report paper focusing on one of the U.S. states. The report had to include the state capital, major cities, state flower, state bird, state motto, major rivers, and so forth. Students would work on this paper all week (mostly at home) and turn it in on Friday. If you did not turn it in, Mrs. Savage would write a zero next to your name.

Back then, teachers thought in terms of *batches of writing*. Such uniformity and order must have brought a measure of comfort. Every student began and finished at the same time. The teacher could leave on Friday afternoon with a stack of papers neatly tucked in her handbag.

Deadlines are not necessarily a bad thing; indeed, most writers in the real world will say that they are a fact of life. Many writers procrastinate; a deadline can provide a necessary kick in the backside to hasten you to the finish line. But the writing workshop embraces the diverse abilities of young writers. Students read at different rates—why should writing be any different? It's not just about the student's ability to write fast. Some subjects are more complex and involved than others, and take longer to write about.

Imagine summer children frolicking at a water park. They hurtle down one watery chute, and then hurry off to try another. Some kids stand in line, impatiently waiting their turn. Still others move to the side, drying off or warming up. A summer water park is a perpetual-motion machine, a hive of nonstop activity. But synchronized? Kids all doing the same thing in the same way at the same time? Ah, no.

That water park is a good way to envision a healthy writing workshop. In many ways, Day 1 of the workshop is the easiest day because every student starts at the same place. After that it may feel like pandemonium breaking loose because most students will be at different places in their processes:

- Trevor quickly finishes a very short story. A few minutes later he starts a second one.

- Malachy spends the entire period chewing the eraser on his pencil, twisting in his seat, unable to get started. By the end of writing time his paper remains blank.

- Kate and Nina are tucked in a corner of the room, talking and giggling. "We're brainstorming!" they insist, though it looks an awful lot like fooling around.

- Amber works feverishly on what looks like it could be the Great American Novel. Three full pages by the end of the period, and she says she's barely gotten started.

By Day 2 the students will be all over the place. Some will be finishing. I think of those students as slices of toast popping up in a toaster—*I'm done! What do I do now?* Others will continue working on their first drafts. There may be a kid who still hasn't figured out what she wants to write about.

At first blush so much differentiation may feel ragged and impossible to manage. But there's an easy way to do so. Tell your students:

"During writing time we'll spend our time writing. When you think you're done, put your paper in the Finished Writing Bin (over here). Then decide what you want to work on next, and get started."

That's it. Make this clear early on so kids understand that when they're finished working on a story or poem they should start a new piece.

(Note: Teachers have devised various management systems. Instead of using a Finished Writing bin, some teachers have students stow the piece in a Finished Writing folder. Some teachers allow students to quietly read the finished piece to a friend before starting a new one.)

A batch of writing pieces that all begin and finish at the same time? Let go of that notion. Let's recognize that the concept of choice extends to how much time a student wants to invest in a piece of writing. Think back to those kids at the water park. They don't hurtle down a slide, announce: "I'm done," and go get dressed. They rush off to try another slide, and then another. Perhaps they feel ready for a steeper challenge. Or maybe they just want to regroup by floating in the Lazy River. They'll keep doing this until it's time to go home. The same sense of *ongoingness* permeates the workshop, and it's a concept that may be more familiar to children than adults.

"Do it again!" kids beg whenever any activity is fun, engaging, playful, and satisfying. It's up to us to ensure that those conditions flourish in the writing classroom.

Tapping into personal passions and interests is a crucial part of becoming an independent, self-directed, lifelong writer.

—JEN SERRAVALLO

11

The Case for Choice

I nearly named this book *Choice Writing*, a title I hoped might sneakily suggest a double meaning. On the one hand, such a title would suggest quality (choice meat, choice real estate, choice writing) that all educators strive for. But it's more than that. Giving young writers genuine choice is the best way I know to create an environment where they can flourish.

Picture your writing classroom as a stagnant pond. You can't do much if the water is just sitting there, if the energy is dead. Positive things happen when you transform your pond into a creek, when you get that water moving. After you've got the water flowing you can dam up one part, gently redirect the flow, and teach your students without them realizing they're being taught.

You get the water moving in your classroom by encouraging your kids to decide for themselves what to write about. Don Murray reminds us that strong writing begins with "honest, specific, accurate information." When kids pick what to write about, they can supply the specifics, the details, the inside info, the *oomph* that underlies strong writing.

You might start the year by having students make an Idea List or Expert List. These lists should be dynamic rather than static—encourage your kids to add to their lists throughout the year.

Choice in writing includes what to write about, but it's much bigger than that. Students who are truly exercising choice are empowered to make decisions throughout the writing process. This includes, but is not limited to:

- Prewriting strategy to use (or deciding to plunge into the writing without using one)
- Purpose
- Lead
- Organization
- Word choice
- Topic sentence (whether to use one, and if so, where it should go)
- Details to include
- Illustrations (whether to include them)
- Strategy/craft element from today's mini-lesson (whether to utilize it in the piece)
- Tone (serious, angry, humorous)
- Length
- Revisions (how to revise and whether or not to do so)
- The decision to abandon a piece of writing
- The decision about when the piece is finished
- Sharing (whether to share and with whom)

Usually young writers jump at the opportunity to exercise choice, but not always. In some classrooms, you'll find students who seem uncomfortable taking risks, and all choose the same thing: every boy writing about hockey, for instance. Although I wouldn't forbid that (realistically, how can you?) I would let students know that I'm interested in the range and variety of their interests, passions, and obsessions.

Choice is powerful stuff, and it will fuel your writing classroom, but it's not a blank check. I remind students that choice does not include the decision to opt out and do something else when the workshop is running. During gym class we all run around and get sweaty. During writing time everybody writes. But almost everything else—how they go about creating a piece of writing—that's up to them. When you give young writers choice, you are giving them a clear signal: This writing is yours. It's part of you. You've got skin in this game.

Students can create ongoing lists of ideas for their writing.

(left: from Megan Sloan's third-grade classroom in Snohomish School District, WA; below: from Ann Marie Krier's third-grade classroom at Chestnutwold School, Ardmore, PA)

Writing can be scary.
Sometimes while you're writing,
you discover that your apparently safe
topic has a hidden trapdoor leading
down to a dusty underbarn you would
have preferred to stay out of.

—R.F.

12

The Burnt-and-Broken Cookie Plate

For 20-some years my wife, JoAnn, and her dear friend Martha have gotten together in mid-December to bake Christmas cookies. This is a four-day, full-blown, no-holds-barred affair. The kitchen fills with delicious smells, rapid-fire conversation, and raucous laughter. But these women are not fooling around. Their shopping list includes 10 pounds of dark chocolate imported from Belgium, and 15 pounds of unsalted butter.

'Nuff said!

During this marathon event I often slip into the kitchen to wash dishes, er, well, that's my cover story, though of course I have ulterior motives. I'm there to spy, to hungrily eyeball the cookies that emerge from the oven trailing heavenly aromas in their wake. There are particular rules governing these delectable treats, and who gets to eat them. The perfectly shaped and cooked cookies are off-limits; I'm not allowed to touch them. After the cookies have cooled they get stacked in large tins; later they'll be sent or delivered to lucky friends and relatives. Does that mean I'm shut out of the action?

Nope. Lucky for me there's a special platter known as the burnt-and-broken cookie plate. This is where the misfit cookies end up, the ones that crumble, the gingerbread man with a missing arm, the angel who stayed in the oven two minutes too long. I can help myself to any cookie on this plate—which I do! True, they're misshapen, often extra-crispy, but I've come to love them.

The burnt-and-broken cookie plate feels like a promising subject to write about. A topic like this is:

- something most people can all relate to.
- humorous (or potentially funny).
- both small and big.

The burnt-and-broken cookie plate contains sensory detail, but at the same time it embodies familiar truths about family, rituals, and how we present ourselves to the world.

What makes a promising topic? It's hard to say. There's no simple formula. I look for ideas that contain rich detail—as well as the possibility of surprise. It should feel authentic and true even if I'm making it up.

Also: I look for an idea that intrigues or mystifies me…where I haven't entirely figured it out. That way I might make a discovery in the act of writing.

Choice is empowering for young writers; however, some kids will be intimidated by it. Students who have had a steady diet of assigned topics may feel unsettled and confused by the invitation to choose what to write about. We need to show students how to "read the world" (a concept I'm borrowing from Donald Graves) so they can find worthy topics to write about.

Spend a few minutes modeling manageable topics from your own life. Students may have the mistaken idea that momentous events are the only ones worth writing about: seeing the aurora borealis in Iceland, meeting the U.S. President, getting caught in a fierce windstorm while sailing on the Chesapeake Bay. In fact, some of the best topics are everyday things that anyone can relate to: burnt Christmas cookies, the junk drawer in the kitchen, the last time you climbed into bed with your parents during a thunderstorm, or saying goodbye to someone special.

When my son Robert went to college he chose a school on the other side of the country. We flew out to help him move in—my wife, my 15-year-old son, Joseph, and me. Robert had chosen a single room, and it didn't take long before we all felt claustrophobic in that tiny space. After 45 minutes it seemed like time to leave.

Still, I felt reluctant. Where would he put his dirty laundry? His extra shoes?

"Where are you going to hang your bathrobe?" I fretted.

"I don't know," he muttered, glancing around. "Somewhere."

"I could mount a hook on the back of your door," I suggested. "You could hang it there."

At this point Joseph put his hand on my shoulder.

"You've got to let him go, Dad," he murmured quietly.

He was being playful, but not entirely. I glanced over at my wife; her eyes were shining. I guess mine were, too.

'Nuff said.

I only write when inspiration strikes. Fortunately it strikes at nine every morning.

—HERMAN WOUK

13

The First Day

Friends of mine started a nonprofit organization. I could scarcely believe all the steps they went through to get their operation up and running. First they announced it via social media (Facebook, Twitter, Instagram). Next they sent out an email blast with more details about their new company. Meanwhile they applied for 503b nonprofit status. When that came through a few months later they promptly announced that as well, reminding people that they could now get a tax write-off if they donated to the new company. In the following weeks they continued building excitement, posting about the latest developments, citing additions to their board, highlighting people who had made donations. Finally they held a "soft launch" followed by a "hard launch." Believe it or not, they were officially open for business.

Kicking off your writing workshop doesn't have to be as complicated as all that. You don't need an elaborate windup. Just begin. The routines of the workshop shouldn't vary—on the first day or every day.

Gather the kids on the rug. If you work with older kids it may feel more natural to let them stay at their desks. Either way, start by giving them a quick pep talk. Note that I said *quick*: five(ish) minutes, no more. Beware that you don't talk the energy out of the writing classroom, something I confess I've done myself a few times.

Share a few possible writing ideas that are kicking around in your head. Ask them to consider what they might want to write about. I often give students 30 or 45 seconds to verbally share with a friend what they're thinking of writing about. Talking and listening helps prime the pump, and makes it more likely they'll have something to write about.

Then send them off to write.

That's it.

Kids should spend the lion's share of the workshop writing. Not talking about writing, not planning to write, but writing. This reflects one of my core values: Kids learn to write by writing about what matters to them, and by living in a community of writers.

Don't be surprised if it takes kids a few minutes to settle into their writing routine. As I said earlier, you can facilitate the proper ambience by sitting at a desk and writing along with them. This reinforces the image of what quiet, sustained writing looks like. Work on your personal writing for five or so minutes. Then get up quietly and start moving around the classroom. Make yourself available to chat with your students.

Give them about a half hour to write.

At the end of the writing time, encourage a few kids to share what they have written. If students have written a lot it won't be feasible for everyone to share to the whole class. In that case I usually suggest that kids read an excerpt. (I've had great results by asking each writer in the class to share one sentence.) If it feels right, and you have time, share a bit of what you have written.

Try to maintain a tone that is positive and celebratory. It's not a contest to see who's the best writer in the class.

Hey, you did it—you survived Day 1!

A student from Megan Sloan's third-grade class in Snohomish School District, WA, shares his writing with a peer.

PART THREE

Writing Workshop: Vital Components

*Conferring is simply
a conversation with another writer.
Let's not make it more complicated
than it needs to be.*

—RUTH AYRES

Conferring With Kids

The writing time is the most important part of the workshop. So what do you do while they're writing? You write for the first five to seven minutes, but then what? Sit at your desk and twiddle your thumbs while secretly checking your email? A better use of your time would be to move around the room and make yourself available for brief, individual writing conferences.

The writing conference is an essential part of the workshop, and I'm an enthusiastic proponent. A chance to work one-on-one with young writers on writing they have chosen to write about? Heck, yeah! That's what drew me to education in the first place.

The phrase *writing conference* may sound overly formal, but it's really no more than an ongoing conversation. A writing conference often begins with you asking an open-ended question like one of the following:

- How's it going?
- What are you writing about?
- Can you tell me about any snags or problems you're running into?

Then: listen. The purpose of a writing conference is not for you to solve their problems for them; rather, you want to help them think it through so they can solve their own.

Imagine a young writer, a fourth grader named Anwyn. Your conferences with Anwyn will evolve during the course of the year. At the beginning of the year you could use the conference

Ralph on Writing
scholastic.com/
WritingCompanion
Resources

to get to know her as a writer: preferences, books that influence her, subjects she likes to write about, how she drafts, the part of the process where she often gets stuck, and so forth. As the year progresses, you'll know when to nudge Anwyn during a writing conference. At some point you may want to have a goal-setting conference, a time when you give her something to shoot for.

During a writing conference, pay close attention to nonverbal clues. Does Anwyn seem like a confident or self-critical writer? What does her body language tell you? Getting a sense of Anwyn as a writer will help you ask better questions during your conferences and, as the year progresses, give her a strategic nudge or challenge.

Much has been written about the writing conference (see Appendix). Remember that there's no one way of conferring. Every teacher must find his or her own way. You will have to find a style/approach that fits your personality. Here are a few suggestions:

- These interactions should be brief, no more than a few minutes. Don't feel like you have to solve all their writing problems. Learn to make a graceful exit: "Okay, I'll be curious to see about how you decide to end your story."

- Don't expect to touch base with each student in your class. That won't happen. Conferring with one-third of your class per writing workshop is a realistic goal to shoot for.

- Crouch or kneel next to students when you confer with them. A stool on rollers can be helpful for those of us with creaky knees or balky backs. In classrooms, teachers often confer with students at the teacher's desk, but I'd suggest you confer with students at their own desks. That way other kids in the vicinity get to hear rich talk about writing. These "second-hand conferences" can be surprisingly influential.

- You don't always have to read the students' writing. You might opt to read one part. Or you could just talk about the piece.

- Be flexible. Follow the conversation where it takes you.

- During the conference you might refer back to the craft element that you taught during the mini-lesson, if that seems applicable.

- **Build on strengths. Make sure to find something the writer has done well, and point it out. I believe you can grow strong writers if you do nothing more than point out what they have done well, and name it for them. Once you name it, they can own it.**

One teacher told me this: "When I confer with my students I try to give each one of them a *glow* (something they're doing well) and a *grow* (something I want them to work on)."

Although I generally endorse the sentiment behind this idea, I don't think it applies to every single conference. In some conferences we do no more than touch base, see how a student is doing, and move on.

Also, we need to be careful of the language we use in a writing conference. Often we phrase our comment like this: "You wrote a strong lead that really drew me in. I could really picture it! But it seems like you kind of ran out of gas in the middle of your story…."

But is the troublesome word here. *But* has a way of erasing whatever came before it. It makes the student focus only on what he or she needs to improve. A better way to phrase there might involve switching *but* to *and*.

"You wrote a strong lead that really drew me in. I could really picture it! *And* I'm wondering if you could do the same thing in the middle of your story…." A subtle difference in your language can make it more likely the student will listen to you.

One more thing: Be sure to respond to their writing as a human being. If it's funny, laugh. If it's sad, let the student know you feel that sadness. First and foremost, writing is a form of communication. If you want to affect somebody, you have to let that person, and that person's writing, affect you first. Let him see that you are genuinely interested in what he's writing. When you do that you open his "window" a crack, and create space for a genuine dialogue.

If the nails are weak,
your house will collapse.
If your verbs are weak and
your syntax is rickety,
your sentences will fall apart.

—WILLIAM ZINSSER (2001, p. 19)

The Mini-Lesson

Have you ever been a soccer coach for a bunch of little kids? They show up for practice after being cooped up in school all day, cranked up on adrenaline, peppering you with questions, rarin' to go. *When can we play? Can me and Kaitlyn be on the same team?* With sophisticated cat-herding skills, you manage to gather them together in a ragged circle. They sit on the ground, staring at you expectantly.

A teachable moment? Possibly, but you better keep it short because those kids are itching to play. A smart coach will give them one thing to think about, and send them off to scrimmage.

Most teachers begin the writing workshop with a mini-lesson. Imagine it as a pep talk you might give to those twitchy soccer players. The mini-lesson builds on their natural energy to create. This is our opportunity to give them one strategy to consider before they run off to start writing. Early in the year you can use the mini-lesson to reinforce routines for the workshop:

- How to use the writing center
- What to do when you're finished
- How to use the editing checklist
- How to manage peer writing conferences.

As the year progresses, you can salt in mini-lessons about the writer's craft (see Chapter 18). A mini-lesson has a short duration, so one might think that planning one should be easy. But some teachers find them intimidating.

"Mini-lessons are hard for me," one teacher confessed. "I feel pressure to come up with a strong lesson to help my students, the perfect strategy to make their writing 'pop.' But often I can't think of anything."

Relax. Take a breath. The mini-lesson shouldn't stress you out. Here are a few tips:

- Keep the tone positive. You want to communicate this attitude: *You're already strong writers, and this idea will help you make your writing even better.*

- Use the mini-lesson to celebrate snippets of your students' writing: "Listen to the way Xander described the delicious sandwiches his grandfather makes whenever they go fishing…."

- How about punctuation, paragraphing, and grammar? Sure, but these issues shouldn't dominate the mini-lesson. Every two weeks or so, you might devote a mini-lesson to teaching a GUMS (grammar, usage, mechanics, and spelling) subskill, such as paragraphing (see Chapter 26).

- When in doubt, use the mini-lesson as an opportunity to read aloud wonderful literature. I'll say more on this in the next chapter.

The last thing you want to do in a mini-lesson is kill the energy, the child's natural desire to write. It's the appetizer, not the main course. Keep it short. In the spirit of brevity I'll end this chapter here.

A mini-lesson about a specific strategy is a good way to begin a writing workshop.

If you call yourself a writer,
you should be reading
like a maniac.

—SHERMAN ALEXIE

Literature That Inspires

As a young writer, I was inspired by Jack Kerouac, Ken Kesey, Jack London, Wallace Stegner, Gary Snyder.... I devoured books like *Kon-Tiki*, *The Ox-Bow Incident*, *The Jungle* by Upton Sinclair, as well as the poetry of Elizabeth Bishop, Gary Snyder, Mae Swenson, and Lawrence Ferlinghetti.

These writers inspired me. Blew my mind. They expanded my horizons by giving me a sense of what was possible when a person sits down to write. They raised the stakes, too, making me impatient with the mediocre (or so it seemed to me) poems and stories I had been writing.

No writer can work in a vacuum. That's why all writers are readers. They have to be. And your students are no different. They need to hear language used skillfully by master writers.

The word *literature* in this chapter title may conjure up images of Newbery Award winners and highbrow works, but that's misleading. By *literature* I mean any kind of writing that inspires students. This includes not only poetry, picture books, and novels, but also spoofs, song lyrics, recipes, letters to the editor, graphic novels, a first-person account of a hunting accident, or a profile of LeBron James.

Having a teacher read aloud to kids during writing time may raise a few eyebrows—*shouldn't they be writing instead of listening to a story?*—but it really is essential. **The writing in a classroom can only be as good as the literature that supports and surrounds and buoys it up. Reading aloud is an essential way to build vision in your students for what strong writing looks like, sounds like, and feels like.** The mini-lesson provides the perfect opportunity to read to your students.

Of course, writing time cannot be the only time you're reading aloud. The strongest support for the writing workshop comes from sharing books *outside* the workshop. Strong writing teachers draw on those experiences when they teach writing. When you do share a book with students, make time for them to respond to the content of the writing before you delve into the craft of the writing. Yes, you'll want to shift their focus from content to craft, but don't make it too quickly. Often that shift comes on a second, or even a third, reading of the book.

So . . . what texts to choose? Young writers need two kinds of literature: one to model a specific technique or craft element, and one chosen for the WOW factor—in other words, for general inspiration. Look for evocative micro-texts short enough to be read in one sitting: poems, passages, picture books, and brief articles.

- Read the text aloud. If it's very short, read it twice.

- Make time for conversation. Encourage your kids to react and discuss the piece without too much guidance on your part.

- Ask your kids: "What did you notice? What surprised you? What do you admire about the way she wrote it?"

- Point out one aspect of craft: "You might have noticed that this poet ended with the same line he used to start the poem . . . ."

- Make the link between what this author has done and the writing students are doing in your class: "Today when you write you might want to consider using this circular structure in your poem. It doesn't work with all poems, but it can be a great way to bring closure to what you are writing."

In any classroom the air will tend to become stagnant and stale. Bringing in lively literature via the read-aloud is the best way I know to throw open the windows and let in a blast of invigorating fresh air. However, we must be patient, and not expect to see immediate evidence that the students' writing has been transformed by what literature we expose them to. Reading will impact their writing, sure enough, but it won't happen overnight. The seeds you plant need time to germinate. Case in point: A few years ago, I was walking through the second-grade wing in an elementary school when a small boy popped out of his classroom. His face lit up; he recognized me from the morning assembly.

"We read your book *Twilight Comes Twice*!" he blurted. "You got beautiful language in there!"

His eyes shone with admiration. It felt like a special moment. In his own way this boy seemed to be saying: "Maybe I can't do what you did…but I can hear it. And if I can hear it I'm building the road inside myself. Someday—maybe not today, maybe not even this year—but someday I'll do what you did, and travel that road, and make a piece of writing that's strong and lasting and beautiful."

*I can shake off everything
as I write, my sorrows disappear,
my courage is reborn.*

—ANNE FRANK

Audience & Purpose

What is writing? Here's my stab at a workable definition: Writing involves selecting particular words and putting them in a particular order to create the effect you want. If you can learn how to do that well, you've got a powerful tool that nobody can ever take away from you.

What kind of effect do you want to create? This depends on your purpose. It has been said that there are four main purposes writers use for writing:

- To express oneself
- To provide information
- To persuade
- To create a literary work

This sounds neat and tidy. I would expand on these basic four and include the desire to:

- entertain others (or yourself).
- remember something you don't want to forget.
- play with an idea, perhaps in a writer's notebook.
- complain.
- express emotion: outrage, love, admiration.
- seek clarification: "I don't understand why...."

- evaluate.

- figure something out.

- wonder, muse, ruminate, doodle, goof around....

Sometimes we have multiple purposes for writing. Let's say that you have dinner at a restaurant. Afterward you decide to email a note to the restaurant owner.

> *Dear Mr. DiSimone,*
>
> *My family and I dined at your restaurant last Saturday night. We had Alana as our waitress. She was so patient with my father (who can't hear very well). Later, my young son left his toy truck under his chair. Alana found it and ran two blocks (in the rain!) to give it back to him. We all agreed that the food was delicious—the eggplant parmigiana melted in my mouth! My only dissatisfaction involved the entrees. I have become a vegetarian in the past years, and I was disappointed that the eggplant was the only vegetarian option on your menu. I'd be grateful if you could consider adding a few more. Anyway, it was a memorable night...and we will certainly be back!*

There were several reasons for writing this note including the desire to:

- praise the quality of the food.

- commend a wonderful waitress.

- tell a brief anecdote.

- persuade the owner to consider including more vegetarian options on the menu.

Although purpose and audience are not identical, they are closely related. And one influences the other. When my son Joseph was in fourth grade, teachers at his school built Mo' Sugar Shack, a small, stand-alone building, to make genuine New Hampshire maple syrup. Everybody got swept up in this exciting project.

And it naturally sparked a great deal of writing for numerous purposes:

- Articles for the local newspaper
- Advertisements to sell the syrup
- Notes to the principal requesting more time to gather sap
- Blog posts to other students explaining the process
- Recipes for foods that could be made from maple syrup
- Fiction incorporating nonfiction bits of syrup-making
- Poems about syrup-making
- FAQ pamphlet for parents
- A how-to booklet for kindergarten students

In every case, the audience for the writing influenced its final writing: word choice, level of complexity, text features, illustrations, and so forth.

Purpose/audience is a powerful duo. What is your purpose in writing this? Who do you hope will read it? Every writer must answer these important questions. But too often it is the teacher who determines the purpose for the writing, so these questions becomes moot. That's unfortunate. We need to empower kids to decide what their writing is for (purpose), and whom they want to read it (audience). If they do, they will experience how decisions about audience and purpose ultimately shape the final writing.

I wrestled with these questions in writing this book. Every sentence is aimed at my primary audience: writing teachers. Not professional writers, not researchers, not academic scholars— writing teachers. I want to speak to them, to you. I'm striving to provide a mixture of inspiration and practical suggestions that will help you survive and flourish during a year of teaching writing.

Writing teachers draw upon three distinct areas of expertise. We must know our students. We must know how to teach. But it's important that we know something about writing itself.

—R.F.

The Craft of Writing

Question: Can writing be taught?

Answer: Absolutely.

And yet the idea persists that writing is one of those things that cannot be taught. How many times have we heard someone say:

- "She's a born singer."
- "He's a born athlete."
- "She's a born writer."

Although these remarks are meant to be compliments, they include an underlying assumption that talent is innate. You're born with it, like height for a basketball player. Either you've got it, or you don't. If that were true, wouldn't it be a waste of time to teach skills in this area?

Certified genius may be one of those gifts you receive at birth, but that's very rare. Most of us are not born anything. We have to work at our craft. We improve slowly over time. That's the kind of writer I am.

In an earlier chapter, I put forth the idea that we don't teach kids to write so much as create a space where they can teach themselves. That's true, but only to a point. Your instruction will have a big impact on helping your students grow as writers. The workshop is the place to start teaching them the nuts and bolts of writing. Writers of every age can start learning strategies and craft elements, including:

- The lead
- Using specific details (instead of vague generalities)
- Bringing alive a character
- Slowing down a crucial moment
- Setting the mood
- Using flashback
- Describing via the five senses
- Creating a mental picture (image) for the reader
- Crafting an effective ending
- Illustrations
- Incorporating surprise

What you teach to your students shouldn't be random, or arbitrarily pulled from a curriculum resource. Ideally, what you teach should be based on what you notice about your students' writing. During your conferences, get in the habit of taking notes about what you notice about their writing, and what strategies might help strengthen it. Smart writing teachers are doing this all the time, and it need not be burdensome. This kind of ongoing assessment should feel natural, like the ebb (what you notice) and flow (what you teach as a result) of waves at the beach.

Ebb: Their pieces almost always begin the same way.

Flow: Show them different kinds of leads.

Ebb: Their stories are plot driven.

Flow: Show them techniques for making their characters come alive.

Ebb: Their writing is flat and predictable.

Flow: Show them how a surprise or unexpected twist can liven up a piece of writing.

Ebb: Their writing lacks depth. As a reader I'm left thinking, "So what? Why are you writing about this?"

Flow: Show them examples of writers exploring important or difficult issues.

When do you teach the writer's craft? You can teach craft lessons to the whole class during the mini-lesson. You can also teach a strategy tailored to a specific writer during a writing conference.

Teaching the writer's craft isn't always easy. Talking about craft may feel a little awkward…like trying to finagle a slippery eel into a narrow bottle. (Many educators have told me they were never trained to teach the writer's craft.) You'll get comfortable with practice and as you deepen your knowledge about writing. In the next chapter we'll look at exactly how I might teach one useful writing strategy.

Quoth the Raven "Nevermore."

—EDGAR ALLEN POE

Spotlight on Craft: The Recurring Line

The recurring line is one strategy that comes in handy with various kinds of writing, particularly poetry. Here's one way to teach it. For this lesson I am indebted to Suzanne Whaley, my friend and literacy teacher extraordinaire.

On one day, read to your class *Grandpa Never Lies*. If possible, read an actual copy of this picture book; the illustrations by Harvey Stevenson are marvelous. (If you can't get your hands on the book itself, the text can be found in the Appendix.) Reading this book may prompt your students to share stories and memories of their grandparents.

You can find the text for *Grandpa Never Lies* on pages 168–170 and on scholastic.com/ WritingCompanionResources.

On a different day, reread *Grandpa Never Lies*. You might start by saying:

> *The other day we read* Grandpa Never Lies. *This morning I'm going to reread it. You already know what the book is about. Today I want you to pay attention to something special the author does in the writing.*

Read the book.

You probably noticed that one line gets repeated throughout the book: "Grandpa never lies, so I know it's true." When a line gets repeated like that, we call it a recurring line.

Have you ever seen a snowball rolling down a hill? Maybe you've seen it in a cartoon. What happens? As it rolls downhill, the snowball gathers more snow. As it does, the snowball gets bigger and bigger. Think of a recurring line as sort of the same thing. As the line gets repeated throughout the piece, it gathers more "snow"—more weight and importance to what you're writing. The last time you hear that line—POW!—it has a really strong impact.

The recurring line is a kind of pattern. The line that repeats usually shows up three, four, five, or more times in the writing, so it can work as a kind of glue that holds the writing together.

If you like this strategy you might consider trying it in a piece that you're writing, just like Ralph Fletcher did. You don't want to pick just any old line. Choose an important line, and then find a way to have that line repeat.

One word of caution: The recurring line is a powerful idea, but it won't work in every piece of writing. It's just one tool I want you to be aware of.

Send the kids off to write. Notice if any students decide to try this idea. Later, during share time, invite at least one of those students to read his or her piece aloud.

Note: *Grandpa Never Lies* is a great book to use if you want to model the recurring line, but this picture book can also be used to model several other elements of craft as well, including:

- Figurative language ("diamonds dancing all over the lawn")

- Strong emotion

- Focus

- Surprise

- Mood

When you look for good books to teach the craft of writing, you don't need hundreds of them; you just need a few dozen books that you know well.

*I'm sure a beautiful
empty notebook was the reason
I wrote my first book.
It was begging for filling.*

—JACQUELINE JACKSON

Playing in a Writer's Notebook

"My teacher says I'm the best writer in the class," the fifth grader wrote to me. "Right now I'm working on my first book. Can you tell me how I can get it published?"

I receive more letters and emails like this than you might imagine. And as much as I admired this girl's enthusiasm and chutzpah, I did feel the need to provide a reality check. I started by gently pointing out that it's unrealistic for an 11-year-old to score a publishing contract.

"Look for local places to publish your work," I suggested. "Think about the school or local newspaper. Publish it yourself and pass it around to family and friends. Don't focus too much on getting published or winning prizes. Now is the time for you to play, to experiment, to try short pieces of every kind. And start keeping a writer's notebook."

I've written a great deal about the writer's notebook and I strongly recommend it, particularly for grades three to eight. (Check out the resources listed in the Appendix.) **The notebook is a high-comfort, low-risk place, conditions that make it a hothouse for writing. The writer's notebook is not a program. It's really nothing but a blank book, but those pages give kids unparalleled space and time and freedom to find their stride and start living the writerly life.**

In recent years, play has been largely banished from the writing classroom. That's unfortunate because children need to play with language in order to grow into strong, confident writers. I think of the notebook as a playground, a place to play with language in countless ways. Students can use their notebooks to experiment by writing notes, sketches, doodles, spoofs, jokes, poems, limericks, cartoons, songs, raps, plays, ads, memes, banners, or bumper stickers.

Kids are collectors. I often remind students that a notebook is a great place to collect cool stuff, including dreams, facts, expressions and figures of speech, sports stats, photos, peculiar articles, and menus with misspellings.

Dear Ralph Fletcher,

One purpose of a Writer's Notebook is to catch (dreams) in a sticky web. To catch feelings, imagination, and sight. Be anyone you want or any thing you want. In short a Writer's Notebook is your passport to a whole new world of fun and feelings.

So strap on your seatbelt and hold on tight I show you some of the best things in my Writer's Notebooks or may have started in Writer's Notebook.

When I get an idea for a story, I usually start by jotting it in my writer's notebook. I don't worry about spelling; I just write it down in its raw form. There—got it! Now I don't have to worry that I'll forget it.

I think of this initial writing as planting a seed. Some seeds don't grow (in fact, more often than not they don't), but others do. Most of my books—picture books, poetry collections, memoirs, and novels—first sprouted in my writer's notebook. (See examples from my own writer's notebook on page 21.)

There's a million ways to keep a writer's notebook, and each of your kids will find a slightly different way to do so. One kid will use it to collect powerful moments; one will play with poetry ideas; one will create superheroes. Your students' notebooks should reflect the varied voices and interests of your class. It's a healthy sign if the notebooks in your classroom tend to look different from each other. You want to encourage that uniqueness.

A notebook gives you a place to react to special moments by writing them down. If you don't record those moments they simply vanish into oblivion. A few weeks ago, we were visiting our grandsons in Boston. As we were leaving, Solomon (3) wanted to step outside onto the porch.

"Why?" his mother asked.

"I want to smell the dark," he murmured.

Hearing the surprising use of language is one of the best things about being around young children. If only I could come up with fresh images like that!

I noticed JoAnn smiling at me.

"You're going to write that in your notebook, aren't you?"

"You better believe it," I told her.

And I did.

PART FOUR

What Writers Do When They Write

We need to show students
the invisible stairs
that writers climb from inspiration
to finished product.

—R.F.

21

A Flexible Writing Process

My 15-year-old son, Adam, developed a sore throat that kept him home from school. I spent the day at my desk as I usually do…chipping away at a pile of emails, proposals, and various writing projects. At supper that evening, Adam shook his head in amazement.

"Were you really working today?" he wanted to know. "Because from what I could see you didn't do anything!"

In the information age, much of what we call work remains invisible to the casual observer. That certainly holds true for the work of writing. Writing is not one skill; it encompasses a bundle of skills that are not readily seen. That's why it's important to spend time talking to your students about the strategies writers use, and make them tangible.

In this section we'll briefly explore these processes, trying to make explicit what often stays murky and hidden. **Let's be careful not to present writing to our students as a neat, linear process, because it's anything but. This process of writing is recursive, often random. Everybody is different, so anybody who sits down to write should feel free to customize the process to suit his or her particular needs and preferences.**

Ralph on Writing
scholastic.com/
WritingCompanion
Resources

I write for two hours every morning, but it's what I do the other 22 hours that allows me to do that writing.

—DON MURRAY

22

Prewriting

I 'll admit it: I have a slightly hostile attitude toward prewriting. But before we get to that, let me extol its virtues, or at least acknowledge them. This initial writing stage has also been called brainstorming or rehearsing. It's the activity we undertake leading up to the actual writing itself: making a list, scribbling a phrase or idea as a mental placeholder, sketching images, doodling, trying out a sample chapter for a memoir. J.K. Rowling famously jotted her initial thoughts about Harry Potter on a napkin while sitting in a diner.

Prewriting certainly is an important part of what writers do. As we've already seen, I'm a huge proponent of the writer's notebook, which is in itself a powerful tool for prewriting. Okay, Ralph, so why the attitude?

Because I believe writing teachers overemphasize prewriting, and give it too much weight. It's commonplace for a teacher to impose a single prewriting strategy, format, or worksheet that all students are required to use. Before they start writing, the students must fill out a graphic organizer, web, story map, or outline. Many kids find this requirement tedious. At any rate, it does not reflect best practice or common sense. Kids have a certain amount of "juice" to work on a particular piece of writing—if they spend it all on the prewrite, what will they have left for the writing itself?

A rigid adherence to any one prewriting strategy distorts the creative process. People who rely heavily on prewriting believe that writers are people who first plan out the writing and then execute the plan. But what about discovering what you have to say in the act of writing? A few years ago, Neil Gaiman was the featured speaker at a Young Authors conference. After completing his talk, he took a few questions from the audience.

"Mr. Gaiman, do you plan out your books first?" one girl wanted to know. "Because our teacher says if you don't plan first then you're just winging it."

Gaiman smiled cheerfully. "Well then, I guess I'm winging it!"

I was winging it, more or less, when I began writing this book. It's true that I had a sketchy idea of what I wanted to include, what tone I wanted to use, but not much more than that.

"I can't give you a Table of Contents until I write the chapters," I told my editor. I had to write in order to find out what I had to say. Most writers will tell you something similar, that they are guided by an I'm-figuring-it-out-as-I-go approach, feeling their way down a dark tunnel.

How then should we teach prewriting in the writing classroom? Should we teach it at all? Certainly, yes. Use the mini-lesson to share a variety of prewriting strategies. One day you might show how making a list can help clarify your thinking. Don't talk theoretically about this idea—model it, using a large chart, showing students how you have found it useful.

Ask them to try each strategy—once. Later, during the beginning of share time, you can hark back to the prewriting strategy.

"How many people found this idea helpful?"

Invite kids to share how it helped. Then:

"Great. If you found this strategy helpful, use it again. If not, don't use it."

Try to expand your students' concept of prewriting to include thinking, musing, daydreaming, or chatting with a friend. I have several friends who report that repetitive action such as running or swimming laps seems to get the creative juices flowing. Writers must be receptive to inspiration whenever it strikes.

Prewriting Ideas

- Observe something/someone · Look at a picture/photo
- Have an experience.
- Talk to someone. Tell him/her about something that happened.
- Make a list
- Draw a picture/sketch
- Make a web.
- Circle an idea + add 3 ideas
- Do some research
- Read a book - take notes
- Just start writing!
- Look back at something you've already started writing
- Make a T-Chart

Teachers and students can work together to come up with a list of prewriting ideas.

(from Megan Sloan's third-grade classroom in Snohomish School District, WA)

The first draft is just you
telling yourself the story.

—TERRY PRATCHETT

23

Drafting

Kids need to produce lots of writing. Sheer quantity by itself won't turn them into great writers, but without it they can never assimilate the myriad skills and strategies they'll need in order to write well.

Most children speak volumes of words, but when it comes to writing, their output dwindles to a trickle. Our goal should be to increase *fluency* in writing (just as we are trying to do in reading). Fluency and a risk-taking environment constitute the two foundational beams in the writing classroom.

Encourage fluency when your students are drafting. Take a reflective stance and pay attention to what impedes that fluency so you can help unclog the pipes. Are students jumping up to use the dictionary or thesaurus while they are drafting? This interrupts the flow.

Drafting = writing. This is what the writing workshop is all about. Drafting represents the sweet spot, the marrow, the tenderloin of writing time. But drafting can look messy when students are engrossed in it. You'll notice some students crossing out entire lines or paragraphs; others decide to start over again. At first blush, there doesn't seem to be much to celebrate. For that reason, teachers may have a tendency to devalue it. In fact, creating a rough draft requires a great deal of higher-level thinking.

The student must be able to:

- encode (as opposed to decode) meaning.
- introduce an idea.
- sequence events.
- select (and spell) appropriate words.
- support a main idea with details and examples.
- develop a character.
- create images so the reader can visualize what's going on.
- find the right way to end.
- make it sound like you (voice).

Celebrate fluency when your students are creating their rough drafts, and encourage them to write a lot. There's no reason why a third-, fourth-, fifth-, or sixth-grade student can't write a page, or even a page and a half, during a half hour of writing time. Writing 300 words is a praiseworthy accomplishment, so make sure your students understand that you're paying attention. "I can't believe you wrote that much!" By doing so, they are developing the stamina, the "writing muscles" they will need for stiffer writing challenges that will come in the years ahead.

A writer is someone who writes a lot. Strive to create a classroom where your young writers can do just that. All this quantity will have a direct impact on you, the writing teacher, in one important way: Realistically, you won't be able to read every single story, memoir, poem, or feature article your kids crank out. And that's okay. If you have time to read everything they write, they probably aren't writing enough.

A Writing Kind of Day
by Ralph Fletcher

It is raining today,
a writing kind of day.

Each word hits the page
like a drop in a puddle,
creating a tiny circle

of trembling feeling

that ripples out
and gathers strength
ringing toward the stars

*I don't teach students to write
so much as I teach them how to read
their emerging drafts.*

—DON MURRAY

24

Rereading

"You should be the world's #1 expert on what you have written," I tell students. "That can only happen if you read and reread what you have written. Good writers do this all the time."

Whenever you write, there's always the danger of self-indulgence. Every once in a while it's important to stand back, get some distance, and appraise what you have written. This flipping of roles—switching from writer to reader—is a crucial aspect of writing. When skilled writers reread, they ask themselves what I call *writer's questions*, ones that closely track the questions we ask during a writing conference. These questions include:

- What am I trying to say?
- Have I said it?
- How does it sound?
- Is it working?
- Does my beginning grab the reader?
- Is there a smooth flow from the beginning to the body of the piece?
- Do I wander off the topic? Where?
- Do my characters (and dialogue) seem believable?

- Should I add details or examples to support general statements?
- Is there a critical moment or climax that I rush through too quickly…a place where I need to use slow motion?
- Have I written a satisfying ending?

I reread many drafts of the first picture book I wrote, *Twilight Comes Twice*.

Emphasize how important it is to be constantly asking these writer's questions. Model asking yourself these questions with a piece of your own writing. Any one of these could provide content for a mini-lesson.

Rereading is a crucial part of the process, but many young writers skip it. They are more than happy to hand a story to the teacher and ask: "Is this good? Will you check this?" Don't fall for this. We don't want to corner the market on what makes a good piece of writing. They need practice developing their own criteria.

In a healthy workshop, kids will be engrossed and reading and rereading their drafts. It's a good sign if you look around the room and see them doing that. Georgia Heard says that we want to encourage kids to reread their writing with an "intelligent discontent." I love this phrase and try to keep it in mind because many writers go to extremes when they read their own writing: "It's great!" or "It's terrible…." The truth almost always lies somewhere in between.

*Revision is not corrective,
it's generative, and it's where
we build our writing muscles.*

—JEFF ANDERSON

25

Revising

"I'm not a great writer," I often tell students, "but I'm a really good reviser." It's an important, even pleasurable, part of my process. I love watching the way a story finds its optimal shape, voice, and power through the revision process. Consider the series of revisions I did while making my first picture book, *Twilight Comes Twice*.

1) My first draft was all over the place: twilight in the summer, the winter, the city, the country, the desert, and the Arctic. After talking with my editor, I decided to rewrite the manuscript by focusing on one time (summer) and place (country). I did so and: voila! The writing felt sharper and more immediate.

2) The manuscript I had written had a poetic feel, so I wondered what would happen if I switched from prose to free-verse poetry. I did that and once again—*bingo*. Free-verse poetry seemed like a natural form for such a poetic book.

3) As originally written, the story spanned early morning to night. I decided to switch the text so that it started with evening twilight and ended with the dawn's first light. This change created a joyful ending (the sun coming up) for the story.

True, this anecdote has a happy ending, but it's important to mention that these revisions were not easy for me. In fact, they made me anxious because each one required a leap into the unknown. I was lucky to undertake these revisions under the guidance of a skilled editor who provided the conditions that allowed me to make them. And these revisions really did make a huge difference. Without them, well, my story would have been like a promising photograph that's slightly out of focus.

Teaching revision to young writers is a huge subject. Many authors have devoted entire books to this subject. (For a deeper look at revision, I suggest you check out my recommendations in the Appendix). Instead of going into great depth here, I'll try to make a few key points.

- Build a wall between revision and editing; it's crucial that your students understand the difference. Revision is not about correcting or fixing up—it's a composing process. Revision is not polishing. Rather, it involves reshaping, revamping, adding chunks, cutting sections, switching parts around.

- Try to instill in your students a positive attitude toward revision. Revision is not a way to fix a broken piece of writing; rather, it's a way to honor a really good one.

- Teaching craft lessons will open up possibilities for revision. For example, after you teach a lesson about character development, students can go back and look at how they described a character. What else might they do to make that character come alive for the reader?

Revision is important, sure enough, but let's not get our expectations too high. According to some educators, students are dying to revise everything they write. If only! When it comes to revising their writing, most kids have an I-did-it-I'm-done-I-really-don't-want-to-do-any-more attitude. I've learned that a student's interest in a piece of writing usually has a shelf life that comes with an expiration date. So let's balance our enthusiasm about revision with a realistic view of a student's stamina and attention span. I'm guided by something I heard the poet William Stafford once say.

"When I write something that interests me, I go back and work on it," he said. "If it doesn't interest me, I go on."

Yes. And the same principle should apply to our students. **We should empower young writers to decide *if* they want to revise. And, if they do, they get to decide *how* and *what* revisions they want to make. It's not realistic to expect them to revise everything they write because that's not how writing works. Often you write something that's just okay, nothing special. When that happens, the wisest course of action may be to put it aside and start something new.**

I read it twice so the reader
only has to read it once.

—JEFF ANDERSON

Editing

This chapter is distinct from the one that follows (Publishing), and yet the two are closely affiliated. I almost never check the spelling of the words I jot in my writer's notebook. If I'm writing an entry comparing my newborn son to a baby primate, I simply want to get my ideas down. Why should I bother to see if it should be spelled gorilla or guerrilla? What I write there is private, not meant for public consumption, at least not when it's still in the notebook.

But if I decide to take the writing out of the notebook, if I want to go public with it, the writing should certainly follow the conventions of standardized English. Or as Nancie Atwell puts it: "Good writing should have what readers' eyes expect."

My first book, *Walking Trees*, contained a misspelling during a description of a teacher's cafeteria in a New York City school. I wanted to paint a scene that would come alive for the reader, so I included a description of a tray of fresh watermelon slices, which seemed like a miracle in that grimy place. But when the book got published, instead of a *tray* of watermelon slices, the sentence contained a *try* of watermelon slices. Argh. What bothered me most was the realization that the misspelling would cause the reader to mentally double-clutch and say: "Wait, what?" It would break the mood—jolt the reader out of the vivid and continuous dream of the book.

When we edit our writing, we attend to the mechanics of language: spelling, capitalization, punctuation, paragraphing, subject-verb agreement, and so forth. As you think about how to incorporate editing into your workshop, make sure everyone understands when it's appropriate to do so, e.g., if and when the student has decided to go public. And it's equally important that they understand the difference between revising and editing.

I suggest you introduce editing about two weeks into the school year. Teach your students how to edit their own writing. If we're the only ones correcting writing, well, we're the only ones who get to practice these important skills. Create an editing checklist that's developmentally appropriate for the age of the students you're teaching.

In the weeks and months that follow, you can continue to teach editing skills during the mini-lesson. An individual writing conference gives you an opportunity to teach one or two editing skills. An editing conference should take place when the student has drafted and revised the piece, and wants to go public with it. A few other things to keep in mind:

- Keep the editing checklist short. The longer the list, the more likely it is your students will gloss over it, or ignore it entirely.

- Teach students to reread their writing each time for each skill on the checklist. And remind them that this kind of rereading is different from the way you reread a rough draft.

- If kids are writing on laptops or iPads, have them print out their writing and edit on a paper copy.

- Consider giving students different-colored markers for each skill: editing for capitalization with a red marker, editing for punctuation with a green marker, etc. This makes it fun and encourages them to reread for each skill. This is a useful tool when kids are first learning to edit in grades 2 to 5; they can let go of it when they've learned how to edit.

- Praise them for how many errors they were able to find. You found five editing mistakes—good job. You found eight mistakes—even better!

- **Don't belabor the editing process. Students should give it their best shot, but I wouldn't force them go back again and again to find more mistakes. At some point the most merciful thing is to step in as editor-in-chief and do the final edit yourself.** There's nothing wrong with that—all publishers employ professional proofreaders. And even then, mistakes occasionally get through.

  While editing is important, try not to let those skill lessons crowd out the other issues of craft you want to teach. Here's a rule of thumb: No more than one out of six mini-lessons should focus on editing skills.

- Teach editing skills in the context of their writing. It's one thing if your students can fill out a worksheet, but can they find those errors in their own writing? That must be the acid test.

*I believe that writing
is the way children's voices
come into power.*

—KATHERINE BOMER

Publishing

Recently in the exhibit hall at the NCTE national conference, I saw a new author with her first book. She tried to look professional, to adopt an expression of ironic amusement or detached mystery, but she couldn't quite pull it off. She was so excited she couldn't stop grinning. She reminded me of a young parent…head-over-heels in love with what she had birthed. She beamed shyly, eager for somebody (anybody) to come by to take a peek at the little beauty.

I'm describing a first-time trade author, but the young writers in our classroom will pretty much feel the same way. After all, writing is a means of communication. After all the musing, the drafting, the cutting and adding and tweaking…it's natural to want to share it, to put your writing into the hands of the reader(s) it was intended for. We need to make that happen.

A few thoughts about publishing:

- Not everything should get published. Some writing is personal. And some writing just isn't good enough for publication. That's a hard lesson every writer must learn.

- Student choice extends to what gets published. And although your students should get the final say, it's important to talk with them about the criteria they should use to make that decision. It shouldn't necessarily be your longest, or your neatest, or the story where the illustrations are the prettiest. The pieces that get published should be the ones where the writing is strong.

- **Tie publishing to editing, as discussed in the previous chapter. The moment your kids realize that their writing is going to be read by an outside audience, there should be a collective gulp in the classroom, a dawning understanding that *this has to be good because somebody's going to read it*. Publishing raises the stakes, and that's good. Your students will want the final writing to be as correct and professional looking as possible.**

- Consider holding a splashy publishing event: an Author's Celebration, book party, school-wide author day. Such events can generate even more writing; for example, students might decide to create invitations and send them to relatives.

- See if you can get your hands on a laminating machine so kids can go through the process of making books.

- Think of publishing as *going public* with your writing. This opens the door to a variety of low-key ways to publish, such as having them read to the class next door, or share with kids in a younger grade.

- Help students find a natural audience for what they have written. For instance, they could mail the writing to a relative, or a friend who recently moved away.

- With primary children, consider two categories of publishing: informal and formal. I believe there should be lots of informal publishing—celebrating student writing exactly as they wrote it—with children in grades K, 1, and 2.

- If a student has written about an important social issue, help that student send the final piece to the appropriate person—the President, celebrity, governor, mayor, or principal. When they do that and (hopefully) get a response, they begin to understand that writing has the capacity to impact the world in a way that's unlike anything else.

PART FIVE

A Year of Writing

Teach the writer,
not the writing.

—LUCY CALKINS

Looking at Student Writing

S killed writing teachers develop an ability to look closely at student writing and quickly assess strengths and weaknesses, as well as other aspects of the writing that aren't good or bad. They're just interesting. I thought it would be revealing to show how I would read a few pieces of student writing. Danielle created this first one. She wrote this either in kindergarten or early first grade (I don't know which).

> Danielle 1/28/
> hO I sey.
> Culrdpant.
> in the sgi.
> itmacksa.
> reabow.

Ralph on Writing
scholastic.com/
WritingCompanion
Resources

1) The opening line is what strikes me first: *Ho, I say.* You've got to love the utter unselfconsciousness of primary writers. It's hard to imagine that older (adult) writers would ever begin a poem this way. This piece has strong voice.

2) Next, I notice the line about *culrdpant in the sgi.* Even at this young age, this writer has a great feel for figurative language. This is noteworthy, especially given the fact that most kids are quite literal.

3) The third thing I notice is her language development. She has some sight vocabulary, and in those cases she uses conventional spelling. It's true that she uses developmental writing, but she also has a good sense of individual words. And even her spelling mistakes (*sgi* for *sky*) make a lot of sense.

4) The fourth thing (actually tied for third) I notice is how she uses a period at the end of each line. Once again, her error is an intelligent one. She is taking a risk to use a period, and she knows it comes at the end of something—a line? Sentence? My guess is that her understanding of what a sentence is hasn't completely developed.

Would I teach her how to use a period right away? Not necessarily. But I know I'll want to do so at some time because she's pretty close to being ready to learn it.

I wonder what prompted her to write a poem. Did the teacher talk about poetry? Has she recently read some poetry books? I wonder if she has a passion for this genre…if so, I'd encourage her to write more poems.

Overall assessment: Danielle is a strong, confident writer. She's well on her way.

Dog Cloning and How It Works
by Michael, fourth grade

You wanna know about dog cloning? Well, obviously
you do because your reading this right now. anyways,
the process start's with your dog (if it is dead). Yo have
to put it into a ded burrito and put the dead burrito into

a freezer for a week. You need to take he/she to the vet were the veterenarian will take a DNA sample (like a bit of its flesh). You will have to mail it off to a company that clones dogs. When the dna sample arrives at lab, they will annilize the dna sample and then they will get another dog. they will cut a hole into her, take out the egg, remove what's already in there, and inject your dog's dna inside, finally they will stich up the dog, put her in a cage (which is pretty big) and a few weeks later your little cloned puppy will come and you could pick him up (once he's a few weeks old).

You can see Step By Step on the back:

This how-to piece definitely made me chuckle in several different places. Here are various things I noticed.

First reaction: Is he making this up or is this actually true? (Apparently it is true.) This borders on Ripley's Believe-It-Or-Not.

Although I love all the ghoulish details, some of them are perplexing. A dead burrito? The piece would be stronger if he clarified that. The details give this piece the ring of truth—this author really seems to know what he's writing about.

This is a classic example of boy writing. I was struck by all the dark humor. Notice how the illustrations are used to convey the humor. The first part (the text) seems to stand on its own, but the boy still decided to add the second part, which looks like a graphic novel. I wonder why.

Note the authorial stance. He's not shocked or appalled. He relates this in a matter-of-fact way. He doesn't editorialize. That gives the piece its power.

Although this kid is a strong writer, he makes lots of small mechanical errors. He's in fourth grade so I'd want to help correct those before he takes this writing public.

Michael is another strong writer, and he's comfortable enough to slip into casual vernacular when he feels like it.

Both these pieces of writing had certain things in common. They both use the element of surprise; this reminds us that we don't want writing that is too predictable. Also, both pieces left me with questions for further investigation.

The writing itself can only tell you so much. Lucy is right: "Teach the writer, not the writing." It's crucial to build a portrait of your student writers so you can put their individual pieces in context. Still, there is a place for learning how to assess your kids' writing, and respond appropriately to individual pieces.

Fifth-grade teachers Jim Flanagan and Kevin Giorno of Girard College Residential School in Philadelphia, PA, created this "We All Come From Somewhere: Family Stories" publication with their students. Here's an overview of the project:

The Experiment

By: DeAndre

Boom! There was smoke, glass, and blood everywhere!

When my father was a young boy he thought about being a chemist. Andre Porter mixed some smelly cleaning supplies together in a glass bottle. When he mixed it up it looked like chestnut brown mixed with a crimson red. Back then he never thought anything would happen to him, so that's why he experimented. So anyway, after he mixed the cleaning products he let it sit for five minutes. After it was done sitting, he started shaking it, but it exploded when he was shaking it. His sister Neysa Porter heard his booming scream in pain. His mother Lillian Porter yelled his sister to call the ambulance because he was in extreme pain. His invention caused him to receive not one or two but eight metallic sutures in his face! They were located over the top part of his oily eye. After receiving the sutures Andre insisted that he will never, ever do an experiment with cleaning supplies ever again. And after realizing it could have been worse, he thought to change his dream job to something else.

Later on in my father life he decided he want to join the proud United States Army. At first, his mother Lillian Porter didn't believe he would actually do it. She thought he was

kidding, but he wasn't. Andre was the youngest of eight children, and was spoiled by his parents and other siblings, so he got what he wanted most of the time. The day my father left for boot camp his mother still didn't believe he had signed up. After she realized that her baby boy had enlisted United States Army, she was angry and she immediately called the United States Army to inform them that Andre had enlisted without her permission. My grandmother was told he was of age, and she would basically have to deal with it. But that was not going to stand with Lillian Porter. Still not accepting the answer, she called the American Red Cross, after that Andre was given permission to call his mother. After his mother scolded him he said, "My family did great thing, and now it is my turn to make a name for myself." Then he said "When all is said and done, I will be home." After that they didn't talk for awhile.

Soon he was honorably discharged from the United States Army in 1989. My mother, Monica Jackson, met Andre at Rock Lobster where they both worked in the kitchen preparing food. By the end of the season at Rock Lobster they decided to get married. Philadelphia, the city of brotherly love, had a big promotion celebrating the millennium in the year of 2000. They were trying to get 2000 couples to get married at Center City Convention Center. He suggested that they should get married. My father was so excited that he signed them up so they could be part of the greatest "2000 Millennium Celebration."

This is the story of my brave, proud, and kind father!

In fifth grade this year, we explored the theme of identity and how our identity is rooted in where we come from. We interviewed family members about our history, and collected many wonderful stories. We collected humorous ones, historical ones, and serious ones, in order to learn more about ourselves.

The fifth grade did a superb job interviewing family members, collecting the stories, recording the stories, and editing the stories several times in order to publish that perfect final draft. The hard work paid off, and now we have an amazing document of our rich collective history.

In our stories we get to see the full scope of our lives—the good times, the bad times, the humor, and the pain. And one thing is certain—we all recognized how important our families are to us, how much we love our families, and how much we rely on one another. Enjoy!

—Mr. Flanagan
   and Mr. Giorno

*If you want to ensure
your young writers do not progress,
grade everything they write.*

—KELLY GALLAGHER

29

Assessment & Grading

Composing a tweet on Twitter always presents a challenge for me. It requires me to take a big, nuanced, multi-layered idea and condense it into one or two sentences with no more than 140 characters. A whole lot of richness gets lost in the translation.

Teachers face a similar challenge when it's time to assess young writers. If you pay attention, and take notes during the year, you will know so much about each young writer: challenges they faced, breakthroughs, failures, favorite and least-favorite genres, willingness or unwillingness to revise, etc. How can you possibly squeeze all the information you've gathered into a single grade?

Throughout the year, you'll be watching and learning about the young writers in your class. It's important to find a system to organize what you learn. There's no one way to do this; indeed, teachers have devised many different systems, including:

- Notes taken on an iPad during individual writing conferences. Many teachers set up a file for each student in the class.

- Three-ringed notebooks with a few pages devoted to notes and jottings you make about each student. I know one teacher who takes notes on address labels that peel off so she can put them in the notebook later.

- Nancie Atwell's Status of the Class (see her foundational book *In The Middle*, 2014). This is a great, super-quick way to touch base with each student and find out what he or she will be doing, writing-wise, on that day.

Whatever system you use, it begs the question: What information should you take note of? I suggest balancing hard data (title of piece, genre, volume of writing produced, revisions made, thoroughness of editing) with more subjective assessments such as notes about the student's stamina, his or her engagement/ passion, willingness to take a risk, willingness to help other writers in peer conferences, and so forth.

The adage *Think globally but act locally* applies to grading writing. It's impossible for me to endorse any one system because whatever you decide will be influenced and tailored to reflect your personal style, the district curriculum, traditions of your school, and so forth. Instead of describing one grading system, I'll propose a few guiding principles.

- Make sure students are involved in assessing their work. We shouldn't corner the market in this regard. I know one teacher who:

    - talks to her class about what constitutes strong writing.

    - asks her kids to read through their pieces. She asks them to select two or three pieces that she will grade. "Pick pieces that show your best work and highlight your growth as a writer," she says.

    - asks them to self-assess these pieces of writing. "What did you do well? What are you proud of? If you had more time, what would you have liked to do to improve the piece? What did you learn about writing from writing it?"

grades these pieces of writing. To come up with a final grade, she combines these grades with other factors: quantity of writing, willingness to revise, willingness to try something new, and being a "good citizen" in the writing workshop.

- Consider having students create writing portfolios. A portfolio consists of multiple writing samples, some chosen by the student, others chosen by the teacher. The student includes a reflective letter that describes his or her writing and progress during the year. After the student puts it together, the teacher has a "portfolio conference" with the student. This idea has not thrived in today's data-driven educational world, which seems to have an insatiable appetite for numbers, but many teachers swear by it.

- **Don't grade everything. If you must give a grade, I'd strongly advise you attach the grade to a body of work. We want students to be taking chances in their writing—that's the way they stretch, and ultimately outgrow themselves. But real learning always involves failure. It's counterproductive to penalize a student with a low grade for a piece where he took a chance and tried something new that didn't ultimately work. If we do so, he's unlikely to take a chance in the future.**

Finally, I urge teachers to stay involved when it comes to revising the report card used in your district because these documents can have an exaggerated impact on instruction. Does the report card accurately reflect our values and beliefs about how young writers develop? Or has it become outdated? These are questions we must never stop asking.

Every successful piece of nonfiction should leave the reader with one provocative thought that he or she didn't have before. Not two thoughts, or five—just one.

—WILLIAM ZINSSER, ON WRITING WELL

30

The Genre Study

A well-designed genre study can enliven your workshop and stretch your student writers, both at the same time. After students have written for several weeks, there may come a time when their energy falters. Is it time to stir the pot and give them a new challenge? A genre study may be just what the doctor ordered.

You might introduce it like this: "Today is Monday. Try to finish up what you've been working on. We'll have a celebration on Friday. I'll bring in snacks, and I'm really hoping each one of you will share a piece of your writing. Next Monday we're going to do something a little bit different. We're going to start working on a new kind of writing: _____."

There are many factors to consider when you decide which genre to pick: what your students are clamoring for, the demands of the curriculum, and your own preference and passions. I urge you to avoid make-believe genres that exist only in school. Instead, select forms of writing that can be found in the real world: nonfiction, sports writing, memoir, persuasion, and poetry.

Let's say you want to start a genre study on nonfiction. The mini-lesson provides a natural opportunity to introduce this genre. Show your students a few examples of real-world nonfiction: books, magazine articles, websites, pamphlets, etc.

"We're going to spend a few weeks writing nonfiction. We'll start by thinking about what you're interested in, and what you know a lot about."

Have each of your students make an "expert list," or a list of subjects they are interested in. Give them time to share in pairs and with the whole class.

Embrace choice within the genre study, and try not to judge which topics seem legitimate and which strike you as bogus. I recently worked in a fifth-grade class where one boy's list included:

- dark magic

- superheroes

- Magic cards

- WWE (wrestling)

- how to make a meme

- how to get extra food at Chipotle without paying extra

At first blush these topics may not sound substantial enough for nonfiction... but why not? This list shows where this boy lives—his expertise as well as his passion—so there's a great chance he'll be able to write well about these subjects.

A few other tips for immersing your students in a genre study:

- Keep the same workshop structure (mini-lesson, writing time, and share) that you have been using throughout the year.

- Use the mini-lessons to teach elements of craft specific to the genre (see Appendix for recommended books on teaching various genres).

- Don't front-load the genre by trying to teach too much at the beginning. The content/craft about the genre can come out gradually during a series of mini-lessons.

- Don't limit the share session to only those kids who have finished. For example, during the early phase of a nonfiction genre study, students might talk about their research, problems they're running into, questions they have, someone they interviewed, and what they have learned so far.

- With nonfiction, encourage students to do several smaller pieces instead of one big report.

- Bring in lots of models or mentor texts to show students what skilled writers do in this genre. Talk about the relevant text features so students can build vision for what this genre looks and sounds like.

In recent years, choice has all but disappeared in many writing classrooms. I would finger relentless test-prep as a major culprit, but also the proliferation of whole-class genre studies based on Common Core State Standards. Like Japanese knotwood and other invasive species, these wall-to-wall units or genre studies have taken over the writing curriculum in many districts.

I don't want to demonize the genre study because, as previously stated, there's most definitely a place for it. But I would offer these cautions. With primary children, I would introduce these genre studies sparingly. When young writers are exploring a new genre, we should keep our expectations modest and age-appropriate about what kids can do.

With students in grades 3 to 8, I suggest we balance genre studies with periodic "open cycles"—a time when each student has complete freedom to choose the topic *and* genre (see Appendix for a suggested yearlong writing curriculum). An open genre is like opening the window and letting in a waft of fresh air. It will energize your class by reaffirming the place for student choice in the writing classroom.

Another benefit to the open genre: Students who are using a writer's notebook can have the experience of following a notebook idea (or seed) to the most natural form. That can't happen if genre is always being taught top-down; in other words, if we're always the ones determining the genre for our students.

Nurturing a boy writer begins by forging a strong relationship with him. Find out what he's passionate about: his favorite sport, the rock group on the T-shirt he's wearing, what he loves to collect at home.

—R.F.

31

Engaging Boy Writers

D o you have a student who avoids or resists writing? If so, that student is most likely a boy. The data shows clearly that boys continue to struggle in writing classrooms.

Why? Boys' difficulties with writing have something to do with the scarcity of male teachers. In elementary school the teacher population is overwhelmingly female. This gender gap may make it difficult for teachers to appreciate the sensibility boys bring to writing.

"I never understood the boys," one female teacher admitted. "I didn't really 'get' them until my twin sons were born. Having boys of my own, and seeing how they act, well, that really opened my eyes."

Boy writing is often fueled by irreverent humor that can sound disrespectful to adults. And boys will push the envelope when it comes to violent writing, which gets frowned upon in today's ultra-cautious environment. Boys are far more likely than girls to hear the word *inappropriate* applied to their writing. As a result, boy writers often feel that they have been shut down and censored. Who can blame them?

Mauled by Seagulls by Peter Lee

One horrible day my brother, Mom, and I went to a beach…not knowing what was about to happen.

We set all our supplies in a shady area so we would not get hot (Ironic.)

Then everyone started seeing seagulls flying above the water. All of a sudden they attacked!!! The next thing I knew, food started disappearing, and people and seagulls started screaming. They were screaming so loud I swear my eardrum was about to explode. Seagulls have a high-pitched scream (seagulls are not my favorite bird!).

In the end, the seagulls won this fight. But next time I'm bringing a machete. It might get messy... but it's worth it.

Boy writers face other obstacles as well. Because their fine motor coordination comes in later than girls', they often get marked down for messy penmanship.

The National Association of Education Progress (NAEP) conducts national writing tests for students in fourth, eighth, and twelfth grades. Recently they gathered data about student attitudes toward writing. They asked students to respond to this statement: "Writing is one of my favorite activities." Fifty-three percent of girls responded that they would agree or strongly agree. Only 35 percent of boys indicated that they would agree or strongly agree. Not surprisingly, the NAEP test results showed a striking disparity between how well boys and girls performed in writing, with girls walloping boys by nearly 20 percent.

I have written several books on the subject, so this is a passion of mine, but my concerns are not one-sided. I certainly don't want to push the girls down in order to pull the boys up. Nor do I want to create classrooms that favor boy writers. But I do think teachers could take steps to make the writing classroom boy-friendlier. The items in the following list are designed to nurture boy writers, though it occurs to me that they will boost girl writers as well.

- Give them real choice about *what* to write and *how* to write about it. Try not to judge what they're interested in (even if it makes you want to roll your eyes).

- Show an interest in what your boys are passionate about. These often make great topics for writing.

- Be more accepting of violent writing (with commonsense limits).

- Celebrate the quirky humor in boys' writing. (Humor = Voice)

- Give boys specific praise during writing conferences.

- Don't overwhelm them with too many revision suggestions.

- Don't insist that students revise everything they write.

- Allow boy writers to collaborate with each other.

- **Make room for genres that engage boys: fiction, fantasy, sports writing, spoofs/parodies, comics/graphic novels, nonfiction, etc.**

- Include mentor texts that appeal to boys: *Knucklehead* by Jon Scieszka, for example.

- Don't outlaw drawing. A boy will often rehearse what he's going to write while he's drawing.

- Messy handwriting? Don't take it personally. Boys are doing the best they can. Allow them to use a keyboard when possible.

- Show an interest in the writing boys do at home for fun.

- Boys write for each other. Don't be surprised if boys view other boys as their main audience.

- Get boys excited about writing. Worry about their engagement first; the quality will come later.

Writing well does not begin with teaching students how to write; it begins with teaching students why they should write. Students who are taught to write without being taught the real-world purposes behind authentic writing are much more likely to end up seeing writing as nothing more than a school activity.

—KELLY GALLAGHER FROM *WRITE LIKE THIS* (2011, p. 7)

32

Picks & Pans

In this chapter I'll provide a brief, no-nonsense, down-and-dirty, cut-to-the-chase assessment of various practices in teaching writing. I'm certainly not the ultimate authority on how to teach writing; however, I want readers to know where I stand on these issues. There's no easy way to prioritize them, so I'll list them in alphabetical order.

- **Author's celebration.** Do it! These events create lots of excitement in the building. Also, they will naturally lead to more real-world writing (introductions, invitations, etc.). But don't wait until spring to hold an author's celebration. Schedule a celebration early in the school year so you can reinvest the energy and enthusiasm it creates.

- **Drawing.** Try not to be so suspicious of it. Images play an increasingly important role in literacy and in the world at large. Allow kids to include drawings and illustrations if they enhance their writing. Show students the important writing—captions, for instance—that accompanies visuals.

- **Edgy boy writing.** Be generous with it. This is where boys live. If a boy writes a piece that clearly steps over the line, okay, step in. But try to make the default response a *yes* instead of *no*. Also, beware of the word *inappropriate*, which is a conversation stopper and makes boys feel silenced.

- **Family writing night.** Yes! Invite families to write together, which may be a new experience for many of them. Many parents habitually read to their children, but never write with their children. Writing can become an important glue that holds a school community together.

- **Genre studies or writing units involving the entire class.** Use sparingly. A few genre studies will go a long way. These units should be interspersed with open cycles where students get to choose the topic and the genre.

- **Grading.** Don't grade everything. Make sure students have a chance to self-assess before you put a grade on it.

- **Grammar instruction.** Usage is important. Rather than acting as Grammar Police, show students how grammar and punctuation can open up possibilities in their writing. As much as possible, teach grammar in the context of their writing. Don't focus too much on memorizing names for the parts of speech. Even after publishing 50 books, I swear I couldn't pick an appositive or a dangling modifier out of a police lineup.

- **Journals.** In many classrooms teachers direct students to write in a journal as the day begins. Often the topics are teacher-directed. I prefer having kids keep a writer's notebook or sketchbook (see Chapter 20).

- **Mentor texts.** Absolutely essential. You can't teach writing without them. Remember: It will take time for the power of these texts to be revealed. Read aloud, make time for kids to talk among each other, and read again.

- **Peer conferences.** Yes, but keep them short. And don't expect these student-to-student conferences to result in substantial revision. Kids will give each other a sympathetic reader (which isn't a small thing), but the peer conference is not a substitute for the teacher writing conference.

- **Prewriting.** Don't overdo it. Don't require each student to do the same kind of prewriting. Kids have a finite amount of juice for a topic. We don't want them to spend it on prewriting. Encourage students to find what kinds of prewriting work for them. Don't be surprised if they prefer to plunge in and discover what they have to say in the act of writing.

- **Publishing.** Certainly! But not everything should get published. The student should get to choose which pieces to go public with.

- **Read-alouds.** Yes. Must be a staple in the writing classroom.

- **Revising.** Most kids avoid it like the plague. Be realistic. Let them choose which pieces they want to revise.

- **Rubrics.** There is a case for using rubrics in the writing classroom. They can help make murky issues tangible so students can grasp them. But when you lean too heavily on writing rubrics you risk creating a checklist mentality in your students. Thesis statement? Check. Concluding sentence? Check.

  "Rubrics are about what the writing *has*, not what it *does*," Tom Newkirk notes. I agree. Moreover, a heavy reliance on rubrics will result in writing that sounds the same, not different. Check out *Rethinking Rubrics in Writing Assessment* by Maja Wilson (2006).

- **Spelling.** It's one member of the "Fab Four" (GUMS). It's no more (or less) important than the others. Suggest students do what professional proofreaders do, and reread their piece backward to look for spelling errors.

- **Story starters.** May work against our goal of creating independent writers, so use sparingly. As students come to writing class, I don't want them to be wondering: "What will she have us do today?" Rather, I want them to be thinking of their own topics, and how they can best write about them.

- **Test prep.** Can you spell *buzzkill?* **If you believe you must devote a certain amount of time to this, well, go ahead and do so. But don't sacrifice your writing classroom on the altar of a high-stakes writing test. I recommend no more than one week of test prep in the fall, and one week before the actual test in April.**

- **Vocabulary.** A richness of vocabulary allows the young writer to convey a richness of thought. Building students' vocabulary is a long-term goal. It comes via reading—lots of it.

- **Writing contests.** Mention the writing contest to your students, but make it optional as to whether they want to submit. Strong writers might be motivated to submit writing. It's another valid way to "go public" with their work, but it shouldn't be the only way, because realistically some of your less-skilled students will never place in a writing contest. Make sure students have a variety of ways to honor and celebrate their writing.

Writing Rules

1.) Use soft voices

2) Please don't
interrupt

3) Everybody writes!

Ralph's basic, streamlined,
no-frills writing rules

*A good writing teacher
is both a good host
and a good bouncer.*

—PETER ELBOW

33

Responding to the Skeptics

When you teach your students via a writing workshop you may get pushback from colleagues, parents, or administrators. The workshop model is unfamiliar to many people, and quite different from the way we learned to write. People tend to be suspicious of anything that seems new. With that in mind, I thought it would be helpful to supply language—let's call them talking points— you might use if you find yourself defending this approach.

* * *

We write every day. I'm proud to say that writing is a big part of my classroom.

I want my kids to develop a love of writing. I keep that goal on a short leash, and don't let it stray too far from me.

Am I bullish on choice? You bet. When we go to the library I encourage them to choose books that appeal to them. When they write I want them to choose topics they're interested in. If they're truly interested they'll work harder on it.

Here's my philosophy: They'll learn to write by writing about what matters to them. That's why allowing them to choose their own topics is so essential.

It's all about getting them to buy in, especially early in the year. That's why I go for engagement first—the quality will come later.

I want my kids to discover that writing can be pleasurable, so I try to make the writing workshop enjoyable. But it's not all fun and games. We're working on other goals, too. For instance, I want them to build stamina as writers. And they need to experiment with writing for various audiences.

My kids amaze me with the stuff they write. I swear, some of these kids write better than I do!

I want quality writing—of course!—but quantity is necessary, too. Unless they do a lot of writing they'll never hit their stride as writers.

It hasn't been perfect. I didn't expect it to be. We've had a few hiccups, but I know my kids are serious about writing. They are coming to see themselves as writers. That's the most important thing.

No, writing isn't the only thing in the curriculum, but writing is a part of almost every subject matter. Writing is the glue that holds our class together.

Identity matters a lot. I want my students to be able to say without a moment's hesitation: "I'm a reader and I'm a writer." And mean it.

I think it's important that they can write with confidence, and not freak out when they have a writing assignment. That will help them in middle school, college, and when they're grown up, too. Writing is a skill they'll be using their entire lives.

There's a prevailing idea that writing is a "girl thing." That myth is destructive to boys, but it persists even today. There's lots of data showing that boys struggle with writing. I'm doing everything I can to get my boys into the game. I find it helps to give them a little freedom. Sometimes the boys do push the boundaries…see how much they can get away with. But I'll tell you this: Some of my strongest writers are boys.

We do lots of read-alouds. My kids love it, and the research shows that there's no better way of bringing rich language to children. It's like taking young ballerinas to the New York City Ballet. They need to see what's possible when they write. They need something to shoot for.

I use a great deal of literature (we call them mentor texts) in my writing workshop. I use them to inspire my kids, to show them possibilities, to build vision for what strong writing looks like. We talk a lot about what it means to *read-like-a-writer*. Because they see themselves as writers, they read differently. Because they are making decisions about their own writing, they can speculate intelligently about the decisions professional writers make in creating their books.

"Writing is one of my favorite activities." I want every kid in my class to agree with that sentence.

Is this approach new? Actually, no. The writing workshop model is popular all around the United States, and around the world, too.

Come in and watch us write sometime. Seriously, we'd love to have you. You can write with us, or just hang out and watch. My door is always open.

Unless students see themselves as writers, have the stamina to sit and write, and want to write, it'll be hard to focus on qualities. They've got to practice to improve.

—JEN SERRAVALLO

34

Something for a Rainy Day

In this book I have championed choice. I have affirmed the belief that writing instruction should be consistent with what writers actually do in the real world. I have advocated authentic writing that is infused with pleasure, passion, purpose, and play.

But once in a while it makes sense to switch things up, and try something new. Many professional writers tell me they have benefited from writing exercises, structured assignments that pushed them out of their comfort zone and stretched them as writers. Personally, I approach these exercises with some skepticism, though I must admit that afterward I often end up feeling happy with what I've written. If the energy dips in your writing workshop, try one of these exercises to give your class a boost:

1) Write about your name. Invite your kids to write about their name: first, last, middle. Ask them:

- How do you feel about your name?
- Does your name reflect your personality?
- Do you have a nickname?

- Who were you named after? Is there a story connected to your naming?

- Is your name ever misspelled or mispronounced? How does it feel when someone says your name wrong?

Make sure your students understand they don't have to actually answer these questions. The idea is that thinking about them will help to get the juices flowing as they begin to write. I've had great success with this exercise. It turns out that names are connected to identity. Your students may be surprised to discover they have a lot to say about this topic.

2) The Good Old Days

> Sometimes I remember
> the good old days,
>
> sitting on the kitchen floor
> with my brothers and sister,
>
> each on our own square
> of cool linoleum.
>
> I'm fresh from the bath,
> wearing baseball pajamas.
>
> Mom gives us a cup of milk,
> two cookies, a kiss goodnight.
>
> I still can't imagine
> anything better than that.

A version of this poem was first published ("Bedtime") in my book *Relatively Speaking: Poems About Family*. It harkens back to a time in my life when things felt easier and simpler. I often invite kids to "write off" this poem and create their own version of it. I suggest that they borrow the first two lines and last two lines of my poem. In between they can write anything they want—in any form—about their own lives.

I've been surprised to discover that even small children can get nostalgic for "the good old days." And instead of feeling restricted, many students appreciate being given the "frame" or pattern. In this case the set beginning and ending act as training wheels, giving kids something to hold onto, making it more likely they will have a successful writing experience. It seems like a paradox, but a little bit of structure can sometimes set you free.

3) Where are you a straight-A student? My memoir *Marshfield Dreams: When I Was a Kid* contains a chapter titled "School." This chapter features my brother Jim, a boy who thrived when he played in the forest but struggled in the more restrictive school environment. The chapter ends with these two sentences: "It wasn't fair, but I told myself that the woods would always be the place where Jimmy learned best. In that school he would always be a straight-A student."

I read that chapter to kids, and we talk about it. Then I reread the very last paragraph and invite them to apply it to themselves.

"Is there a place (maybe outside the classroom) where you learn best? A place where you're a straight-A student?"

The purpose of this activity is to encourage kids to tap into non-academic areas where they excel. I have gotten some remarkable pieces of writing:

—"I'm a straight-A student when I babysit my little sister."
—"I'm a straight-A student on my soccer team."
—"I'm a straight-A student when it comes to cracking jokes in church."

When you find yourself writing a lot about a subject, you know you've got a good topic. These three exercises meet that standard. Make sure to allow plenty of time for kids to share what they've written. **Remember: Writing exercises like this do not constitute a curriculum. They should be used judiciously—the exception, not the rule. But exercises like these often can have a tangible upside: increased writing stamina, a greater sense of community, plus a reminder that writing can be fun. Nothing wrong with that!**

Writing is a matter of selecting particular words and putting them in a particular order to create the effect you want. When you teach students how to do that well you give them a powerful tool, and one that nobody can ever take away from them.

—R.F.

35

Closing Time: End-of-the-Year Rituals

As the year winds down, many teachers find it useful to establish a few end-of-the year rituals. These rituals serve both the student and teacher. They allow you and your students to take stock, to see what your students have learned about writing during the course of the year. In addition, they give you a sense of what you have accomplished, and where you might want to go from here.

Don't wait too long to schedule this. Many teachers find that the school year comes to an abrupt end in May or June. Also, end-of-school activities and field trips render many days unuseable in this regard. So whatever ritual you end up using, plan ahead, put it on your calendar, and protect this time so it doesn't get co-opted by something else.

Many teachers give their students an end-of-the-year writing survey that invites them to reflect on the past year. I like one created by Ruth Ayres, author of *Celebrating Writers* (2013):

See pages 173–175 for the end-of-year student reflection forms.

"When students have been in an active workshop for many months, they will become stronger writers," Ruth Ayres says. "If we don't take time to reflect, then we miss an opportunity to see and celebrate their progress. Celebration fuels writers. By taking time at the end of the year to reflect, we build students' confidence as writers and send them on to the next leg of their journey knowing they can become a stronger writer and ready to persevere."

Instead of using a written survey, some teachers devise a ritual for closure and to celebrate what kids have done.

"As we enter the last two to three weeks of school, I gather my writers to talk about all that we've accomplished," explains Dalila Eckstein, a third-grade teacher. "I ask them to think about what they've done that makes them proud as writers. Then I ask them to mark pages that they would be willing to let me copy to share with future third-grade writers. We then gather around the copier while students sticky-note pages and show each other pages they've chosen. The best part of that is when students tell me why they want me to copy a particular page and why it is important to them as a writer. How students interact with each other and reflect on their own work is what cements the message that they are writers. As students talk about the pages they are marking, it jogs the memories of fellow writers who go back through their pages to find something they did like that. It's a pretty exciting moment for the kids because they see how much they've accomplished and in what ways they've grown."

I love this! Dalila has structured an activity that allows her students to reflect on a year of writing. I'm struck by how the writing samples that students select jog each other's memories.

A ritual like this will build community, and cement the feeling of community that's already there.

"Last year, I invited my writers to share with my new class something they wrote over the summer," Dalila adds. "I had three boys this year who asked to share their writing with this year's class, and it became a launch for a discussion about writing for our own purposes. The excitement this generated resulted in a burst of informal writing!"

And what about you? **You have invested a tremendous amount of sweat equity into the writing workshop; what does it all add up to? That's an important question. During those last hectic three or four weeks of school, make time to reflect on your writing workshop and the group of writers with whom you worked.** Give yourself a moment of reflection, and ask yourself:

- What am I proud of?
- What didn't work as well as I hoped?
- When did my students' energy seem to falter?
- When did my energy go down? Is there are a correlation between the two?
- Is there anything I'd do differently, or new challenges I'd like to tackle? Perhaps I'd like to:
  - try a poetry genre study.
  - take steps to make my classroom boy-friendlier.
  - do more of my own writing.
  - schedule more "Open Cycles" for students.

Envision the year that just passed as a rough draft. As you look ahead to next year, ask yourself: How would I like to revise things to create a better, stronger workshop?

We are cups, constantly and quietly being filled. The trick is knowing how to tip ourselves over and let the beautiful stuff out.

—RAY BRADBURY

36

Exit Interview

Q: You're very strong on giving kids as much choice as possible.

A: Yes.

Q: Why do you think teachers resist giving kids choice?

A: I suspect it has something to do with the issue of control. We feel that when we give kids too much choice we will lose control. Then it's a matter of the inmates taking over the asylum (or some other metaphor that's hopefully not too un-PC). But it's a nuanced thing, right? Yes, we do give up *some* control in the writing workshop, but in return we get a lot of genuine engagement. I'd say that's a worthwhile trade.

Q: In many classrooms it takes students a long time, often weeks, to bring one piece of writing from seed idea to finished product. I've heard you tell teachers that students shouldn't belabor a piece of writing. Do I have that right?

A: Glad to see you're paying attention.

Q: What do you mean by that?

A: When I went to school I wrote rarely, but when I did, my teacher tried to get a lot of mileage on that piece of writing. I suggest we reverse that. Teachers should have kids writing frequently, but only try to get a little bit of mileage out of each piece of writing. Squeeze it once and let it go. You may not see evidence of growth while the student is working on one particular piece, but it will show up in a subsequent piece.

Q: You talk about short-term goals and long-term goals.

A: I don't think of them as goals…more like areas to focus on.

Q: All right. I notice your list is pretty short. Some districts break out 30 or 40 goals per grade level.

A: That's too much. Realistically, students are not going to meet 40 writing goals in one school year. Tom Newkirk says that a curriculum should be short enough to fit on a legal-sized envelope. Streamlined. I believe the same thing about writing goals. Let's keep the list short and manageable. If those goals are worthwhile, we will need to revisit them several times during the year.

Q: How is writing changing in the digital world?

A: The jury is still out. On the one hand, writing is still writing. But things are certainly changing, and we'll have to see how it all shakes out. When it comes to technology, I've observed a few troubling things. In one school, a wealthy benefactor made a gift so that every student could have his or her own iPad. After that the district frantically rewrote the writing curriculum around those iPads, making it the centerpiece. That strikes me as backward. Districts should create a strong, enlightened writing curriculum and then see how the available technology can support that curriculum.

Q: **Would you like to see any changes in the writing workshop?**

A: Possibly. I've been thinking about that. Right now silence and stillness are hallmarks of a strong writing classroom. I was the kind of kid who could have flourished in that kind of environment. It does work for many students, but not all. Some students (boys) find the workshop too solitary and static. I'd like to see it become a bit more kinetic. Let kids move around.

Q: **Anything else?**

A: I believe we should be encouraging more collaborative writing…two kids working on a piece about dinosaurs, for example. Many teachers outlaw working with a friend, but why? If it's more social, it's more fun. And businesses tell us they want young people who can work on a team, synthesize information, and write a collective report. In the business world being able to collaborate is a big plus.

Q: **[sighing] It's all about the business world.**

A: No, I'm not saying that. But school should be preparing kids for writing challenges they'll encounter in the rest of their life.

Q: **What is something nobody tells you about teaching writing?**

A: Your students will do a lot of bad writing during the school year. There's no way around it. We all want excellent writing, but a lot of what they produce is just not very good. (That's true for adult writers, as well.) That's the nature of the beast.

Q: A lot of teachers get freaked out by high-stakes testing, so much that they make test prep the centerpiece of their writing instruction.

A: Which is a huge mistake.

Q: You think so?

A: Yes. It's understandable but misguided. A steady diet of test-prep is like feeding your child a diet that lacks the major food groups. It's a form of malnourishment. Plus, kids will hate it. And most of them see through it. Preparing so they'll perform well on a state writing test? We know the payoff for us (adults), but what's the payoff for them? Nothing.

Kids will do just fine on the writing test if they write a lot, if they see themselves as writers, if they write for various purposes, if they have time to play and experiment, if we read aloud powerful literature, if we show them the moves that skilled writers make. And here's the best part: When they walk out of the classroom on the last day of school, they'll see themselves as writers. They'll believe that to their core.

Q: So you are recommending against any test preparation?

A: No, I didn't say that. It would be prudent to do some test prep…perhaps spending a week making sure students are familiar with the test and know what to expect. Let them experience what it's like to write to an assigned prompt. One week is enough.

Q: Any final words of advice for writing teachers?

A: Don't get overwhelmed. **You can get there from here.** Remember that it's not just a process for students—teaching writing is also a process for us. We're in process: pre-teaching, rough drafting, reading the energy of the class, revising, tweaking.... Give yourself permission to screw up once in a while. I certainly did when I got started. You'll learn a ton along the way. Embrace the journey. And have fun!

Appendix

Note: This Appendix begins with a half dozen Seminal Resources for Teaching Writing, books that every writing teacher should be aware of. After that, I provide suggested resources that correlate with the appropriate chapter in this book.

Seminal Resources for Teaching Writing

In The Middle, Third Edition: A Lifetime of Learning About Writing, Reading, and Adolescents by Nancie Atwell. Heinemann. 2014.

The Art of Teaching Writing by Lucy Calkins. Heinemann. 1994.

A Fresh Look at Writing by Donald Graves. Heinemann. 1994.

Writing: Teachers and Children at Work by Donald Graves. Heinemann. 2003.

The Essential Don Murray: Lessons from America's Greatest Writing Teacher by Donald Murray. Edited by Lisa Miller and Tom Newkirk. Heinemann. 2009.

On Writing Well: The Classic Guide to Writing Nonfiction by William Zinsser. Harper Perennial. 2016.

Writing Workshop

Writing Workshop: The Essential Guide by Ralph Fletcher and JoAnn Portalupi. Heinemann. 2001.

The Writing Workshop: Working Through the Hard Parts (and they're all hard parts) by Lester L. Laminack and Katie Wood Ray. Heinemann. 2001.

About the Authors: Writing Workshop with Our Youngest Writers by Katie Wood Ray and Lisa B. Cleaveland. Heinemann. 2004.

Chapter 14: The Writing Conference

Hidden Gems: Naming and Teaching from the Brilliance in Every Student's Writing by Katherine Bomer. Heinemann. 2010.

How's It Going? A Practical Guide to Conferring with Student Writers by Carl Anderson. Heinemann. 2000.

Conferences and Conversations: Listening to the Literate Classroom by Douglas Kaufmann. Heinemann. 2000.

Easy-to-Manage Reading & Writing Conferences (Grades 4–8) by Laura Robb. Scholastic.

Chapter 16: Literature That Inspires

The Writing Thief: Using Mentor Texts to Teach the Craft of Writing by Ruth Culham. International Reading Association. 2014.

Nonfiction Mentor Texts: Teaching Informational Writing Through Children's Literature, K–8 by Lynne R. Dorfman and Rose Cappelli. Stenhouse. 2009.

Mentor Author, Mentor Text: Short Texts, Craft Notes, and Practical Classroom Uses by Ralph Fletcher. Heinemann. 2011.

Write Like This: Teaching Real-World Writing Through Modeling and Mentor Texts by Kelly Gallagher. Stenhouse. 2011.

Wondrous Words: Writers and Writing in the Elementary Classroom by Katie Wood Ray. NCTE. 1999.

Chapter 18: The Craft of Writing

10 Things Every Writer Needs to Know by Jeff Anderson. Stenhouse. 2011.

25 Mini-Lessons for Teaching Writing (Grades 3–6) by Adele Fiderer. Scholastic. 1999.

Craft Lessons: Teaching Writing K–8, Second Edition, by Ralph Fletcher and JoAnn Portalupi. Stenhouse. 2007.

Live Writing: Breathing Life Into Your Words by Ralph Fletcher. HarperCollins. 1999.

The Writing Strategies Book: Your Everything Guide to Developing Skilled Writers by Jen Serravallo. Heinemann. 2017.

Nonfiction Craft Lessons: Teaching Informational Writing K–8 by JoAnn Portalupi and Ralph Fletcher. Stenhouse.

What a Writer Needs, Second Edition by Ralph Fletcher. Heinemann. 2013.

Chapter 19: Spotlight on Craft: The Recurring Line

Grandpa Never Lies by Ralph Fletcher. Illustrated by Harvey Stevenson. Clarion Books.

Grandpa Never Lies

Summers are the best.
I get to spend a whole month at
Grandma and Grandpa's little
house in the woods.

We eat Grandma's blueberry pancakes,
track wild deer,
hunt trilobite fossils,
swim, play cards,
but mostly just talk.

When I ask what happened to Grandpa's hair,
he tells me, "A roaring tornado made me bald—
blew off my hair as it twisted through."

And Grandpa never lies,
so I know it's true.

When I visit on cold fall days,
we drink hot chocolate while Grandpa
reads from a book of fairy tales.

I see on the windows the blooming frost
and ask about those delicate lines.

Grandpa tells me about the winter elves
who come at dusk with magical brushes
to sketch on glass their silvery hues.

And Grandpa never lies,
so I know it's true.

In winter Grandpa and I go on long walks.
We always stop at Tolliver's barn
to pull down wicked icicle swords,
each one filled with sharp clear light,
and challenge each other to a sword fight.

Grandpa tells me
how the wind works at night,
sharpening icicles as they grow.

And Grandpa never lies,
so I know it's so.

Then Grandma died.
Suddenly.
At the funeral I was too shocked to cry.

A month later Grandpa took me ice fishing at night.

He held my hand while we crossed Spy Pond
and showed me how to cut out circles of ice.

When I asked if he missed Grandma

fat young tears rolled down his cheeks.
We could hear the ice settle and moan.

He said: "Ice this deep can talk to you."

And Grandpa never lies, so I know it's true.

It's spring now.
Grandpa's visiting.

We like to wake up, just he and I,
and sneak outside at sunrise while
diamonds dance all over the lawn.

He explains to me how spiders work,
stringing water beads on the finest thread,
decorating their webs with morning dew.

And Grandpa never lies,
so I know it's true.

Mornings we eat cereal on the porch
and make plans for the summer,
when I'll get to spend a whole month
at Grandpa's little house in the woods.

We'll dig for crystals,
sleep under the stars,
swim, play cards,
but mostly just talk.

When he asks me:
"What's your favorite thing?"
I tell him, "Spending time with you."

And I never lie, so Grandpa knows it's true.

Other picture books that use a recurring line:

One Day in the Eucalyptus, Eucalyptus Tree by Daniel Bernstrom. Illustrated by Brendan Wenzel. HarperCollins. 2016.

They All Saw a Cat by Brendan Wenzel. Chronicle Books. 2016.

Chapter 20: Playing in a Writer's Notebook

Notebook Know-How: Strategies for the Writer's Notebook by Aimee Buckner. Stenhouse. 2005.

A Writer's Notebook: Unlocking the Writer Within You by Ralph Fletcher. HarperCollins. 1996

Breathing In, Breathing Out: Keeping a Writer's Notebook by Ralph Fletcher. Heinemann. 1996.

Lessons for the Writer's Notebook by Ralph Fletcher and JoAnn Portalupi. Heinemann. 2005.

Chapter 21: A Flexible Writing Process

How Writers Work: Finding a Process That Works for You by Ralph Fletcher. HarperCollins. 2000.

Chapter 25: Revising

Revision Decisions: Talking Through Sentences and Beyond by Jeff Anderson and Deborah Dean. Stenhouse. 2014.

Is It Done Yet? Teaching Adolescents the Art of Revision by Barry Gilmore. Heinemann. 2017.

The Revision Toolbox: Teaching Techniques That Work, Second Edition by Georgia Heard. Heinemann. 2014.

After The End: Teaching and Learning Creative Revision, Second Edition by Barry Lane. Heinemann. 2015.

Real Revision: Authors' Strategies to Share with Student Writers by Kate Messner. Stenhouse. 2011.

Chapter 26: Editing

Everyday Editing: Inviting Students to Develop Skill and Craft in Writer's Workshop by Jeff Anderson. Stenhouse. 2007.

Mechanically Inclined: Building Grammar, Usage, and Style into Writer's Workshop by Jeff Anderson. Stenhouse. 2005.

Practical Punctuation: Lessons on Rule Making and Rule Breaking in Elementary Writing by Dan Feigelson. Heinemann. 2008.

Chapter 28: Looking at Student Writing

Hidden Gems: Naming and Teaching from the Brilliance in Every Student's Writing by Katherine Bomer. Heinemann. 2010.

Lessons from a Child by Lucy Calkins. Heinemann. 1994.

Teaching the Qualities of Writing by Ralph Fletcher and JoAnn Portalupi. Firsthand/Heinemann. 2008.

Chapter 29: Assessment and Grading

Assessing Writers by Carl Anderson. Heinemann. 2005.

Chapter 30: The Genre Study

Making Nonfiction from Scratch by Ralph Fletcher. Stenhouse. 2016.

Poetry Matters: Writing a Poem from the Inside Out by Ralph Fletcher. HarperCollins. 2002.

Awakening the Heart: Exploring Poetry in Elementary and Middle School by Georgia Heard. Heinemann. 1999.

Study Driven: A Framework for Planning Units of Study in the Writer's Workshop by Katie Wood Ray. Heinemann. 2006.

Chapter 31: Engaging Boy Writers

Boy Writers: Reclaiming Their Voices by Ralph Fletcher. Stenhouse. 2006.

Guy-Write: What Every Guy Writer Needs to Know by Ralph Fletcher. Henry Holt. 2012.

Chapter 35: Closing Time: End-of-the-Year Rituals

_____'s End-of-Year Reflection

MY FAVORITE

Title:	Date:

Rationale:

_____

_____

_____

_____

_____

_____

I LEARNED THE MOST

Title:	Date:

Rationale:

_____

_____

_____

_____

_____

MOST MEANINGFUL

Title:	Date:

Rationale:

_____

_____

_____

_____

_____

_____

I WISH I HAD MORE TIME

Title:	Date:

Rationale:

_____

_____

_____

_____

_____

_____

END-OF-THE-YEAR WRITING SURVEY

(from Tara Smith, sixth-grade teacher, Glen Rock Middle School in Glen Rock, NJ)

Please fill this form out thoughtfully so that I can learn from you and be a better Writing Workshop teacher. :)

1. What changed in the way you choose what to write about this year?

2. Name two ways in which you have grown as a writer this year.

3. What changed in your writing habits this year? Be specific, give examples.

4. Has the amount of writing and variety of writing changed for you this year? What made this possible? Be specific and give examples.

5. What surprised you about your year of writing in sixth grade?

6. What do you know about yourself as a writer now that you didn't know when you began sixth grade?

Index